AVADHŪTA GĪTĀ

(S… …ee)

Translated and annotated

by

SWAMI ASHOKANANDA

SRI RAMAKRISHNA MATH

MYLAPORE : : MADRAS-600004

Published by
The President
Sri Ramakrishna Math
Mylapore, Chennai-4

VIII-2M 3C-1-2009
ISBN 81-7120-037-0

Printed in India at
Sri Ramakrishna Math Printing Press
Mylapore, Chennai-4

FOREWORD

The *Avadhūta Gitā* is a text of Vedanta representing extreme Advaita or Nondualism. It is ascribed to Dattātreya (Datta, son of Atri), who is looked upon as an Incarnation of God. Unfortunately, we possess no historical data concerning when or where he was born, how long he lived, or how he arrived at the knowledge disclosed in the text. Some of the Purānas mention him, and of these, the *Mārkandeya* contains the longest reference; but even this is legendary and by no means very informative.

The account in the *Mārkaṇḍeya Purāna* suggests the following facts of Dattātreyas's life: He was born of highly spiritual parents, Atri and Anasūyā; very early in life he became renowned as a great warrior, and soon, renouncing the world and devoting himself to the practice of yoga, he attained to the highest state of liberation, thus becoming an *avadhūta*.

Avadhūta means a liberated soul, one who has "passed away from" or "shaken off" all worldly attachments and cares and has attained a spiritual state equivalent to the existence of God. Though *avadhūta* naturally implies renunciation, it includes an additional and yet higher state which is neither attachment nor detachment but beyond both. An *avadhūta* feels no need of observing any rules, either secular or religious. He seeks nothing, avoids nothing. He has neither knowledge nor ignorance. Having realized that he is the infinite Self, he lives in that vivid realization. To the Hindu mind, Dattātreya is a symbol of this realization. Whoever the unknown composer of the *Avadhūta Gītā* may have been, he must himself have been a man of the highest spiritual perception.

The *Avadhūta Gītā* is a small book of only eight chapters and is written in spirited Sanskrit verse, which breathes the atmosphere of the highest experience of Brahman. It goes into no philosophical argument to prove the oneness of reality, but is content to make the most startling statements, leaving the seeker of truth to imbibe them and be lifted from illusion into the blazing light of Knowledge (*jñāna*).

Advaita Vedantins have prized this *Gītā* highly. Swami Vivekananda, one of the greatest Advaitins of all time, often quoted from it. He once said, "Men like the one who wrote this Song keep religion alive. They have actually realized; they care for nothing, feel nothing done to the body, care not for heat, cold, danger, or anything. They sit still, enjoying the bliss of Atman, and though red-hot coals burn the body, they feel them not."

The present English translation was first published in part in 1946 in *The Voice of India*, a magazine of the Vedanta Society of Northern California. The learned translator, Swami Ashokananda, a senior monk of the Ramakrishna Order, served as editor of *Prabuddha Bharata* from 1926 to 1931 and was in charge of the Vedanta Society of Northern California from 1932 until his passing away in December of 1969.

CONTENTS

Foreword		... v
Chapter	I	... 1
,,	II	... 40
,,	III	... 64
,,	IV	... 96
,,	V	... 113
,,	VI	... 134
,,	VII	... 152
,,	VIII	... 162

AVADHŪTA GĪTĀ

Chapter I

ईश्वरानुग्रहादेव पुंसामद्वैतवासना ।
महद्भयपरित्राणाद्विप्राणामुपजायते ॥ १ ॥

īśvarānugrahād-eva puṁsām advaita-vāsanā
mahadbhaya-paritrāṇāt viprāṇām upajāyate.

1. Through the grace of God alone, the desire for nonduality arises in wise men to save them from great fear.

Nonduality—monistic Consciousness, in which the knower, knowledge, and knowable—soul and God—become one; the highest realization of Divinity.

Fear—The word "fear" includes also such states of mind as insecurity, despair, and grief, all of which arise from a consciousness of oneself as limited and separate from others and which therefore can be dispelled only by realizing oneself as the All.

येनेदं पूरितं सर्वमात्मनैवात्मनात्मनि ।
निराकारं कथं वन्दे ह्यभिन्नं शिवमव्ययम् ॥ २ ॥

yenedaṁ pūritaṁ sarvam ātmanaivātmanātmani
nirākāraṁ kathaṁ vande hy-abhinnaṁ śivam avyayam

2. How shall I salute the formless Being, indivisible, auspicious, and immutable, who fills all this with His Self and also fills the self with His Self?

Salute—No form of greeting or worship is possible where there is no consciousness of distinction.

Fills, etc.—The reality and substance of the so-called individual self is the Divine Self.

पञ्चभूतात्मकं विश्वं मरीचिजलसन्निभम् ।
कस्याप्यहो नमस्कुर्यामहमेको निरञ्जनः ॥ ३ ॥

pañcabhūtātmakaṁ viśvaṁ marīci-jala-sannibham
kasyāpy-aho namas-kuryām aham eko nirañ-janaḥ.

3. The universe composed of the five elements is like water in a mirage. Oh, to whom shall I make obeisance—I who am one and taintless?

Five elements—earth, water, fire, air, and ether. According to most philosophical systems of India, these combine to constitute the phenomenal universe and are derived from God associated with māyā or ignorance. The terms are not to be taken literally.

Taintless—untouched by the slightest ignorance and hence absolutely pure. The word is often applied to the Self and God.

आत्मैव केवलं सर्वं भेदाभेदो न विद्यते ।
अस्ति नास्ति कथं ब्रूयां विस्मयः प्रतिभाति मे ॥४॥

ātmaiva kevalaṁ sarvaṁ bhedābhedo na vidyate
astināsti kathaṁ brūyāṁ vismayaḥ pratibhāti me.

4. All is verily the absolute Self. Distinction and nondistinction do not exist. How can I say, "It exists; it does not exist"? I am filled with wonder!

It—the universe.

वेदान्तसारसर्वस्वं ज्ञानं विज्ञानमेव च ।
अहमात्मा निराकारः सर्वव्यापी स्वभावतः ॥५॥

vedānta-sāra-sarvasvaṁ jñānaṁ vijñānam eva ca
aham-ātmā nirākāraḥ sarvavyāpī svabhāvataḥ.

5. The essence and the whole of Vedānta is this Knowledge, this supreme Knowledge: that I am by nature the formless, all-pervasive Self.

यो वै सर्वात्मको देवो निष्कलो गगनोपमः ।
स्वभावनिर्मलः शुद्धः स एवाहं न संशयः ॥६॥

yo vai sarvātmako devo niṣkalo gaganopamaḥ
svabhāva-nirmalaḥ śuddaḥ sa evāhaṁ na saṁśayaḥ.

6. There is no doubt that I am that God who is the Self of all, pure, indivisible, like the sky, naturally stainless.

अहमेवाव्ययोऽनन्तः शुद्धविज्ञानविग्रहः ।
सुखं दुःखं न जानामि कथं कस्यापि वर्तते ॥ ७ ॥

aham evāvyayo'nantaḥ śuddha-vijñāna-vigrahaḥ
sukhaṁ duḥkhaṁ na jānāmi kathaṁ kasyāpi vartate.

7. I indeed am immutable and infinite and of the form of pure Intelligence. I do not know how or in relation to whom joy and sorrow exist.

न मानसं कर्म शुभाशुभं मे
न कायिकं कर्म शुभाशुभं मे ।
न वाचिकं कर्म शुभाशुभं मे
ज्ञानामृतं शुद्धमतीन्द्रियोऽहम् ॥ ८ ॥

na mānasaṁ karma śubhāśubhaṁ me
na kāyikaṁ karma śubhāśubhaṁ me
na vācikaṁ karma śubhāśubhaṁ me
jñānāmṛtaṁ śuddham atīndriyo'ham.

8. I have no mental activity, good or bad; I have no bodily function, good or bad; I have no verbal action, good or bad. I am the nectar of Knowledge, beyond the senses, pure.

मनो वै गगनाकारं मनो वै सर्वतोमुखम् ।
मनोऽतीतं मनः सर्वं न मनः परमार्थतः ॥ ९ ॥

mano vai gaganākāraṁ mano vai sarvato mukham
mano'tītaṁ manaḥ sarvaṁ na manaḥ paramārthataḥ.

9. The mind indeed is of the form of space. The mind indeed is omnifaced. The mind is the past. The mind is all. But in reality there is no mind.

All—the phenomenal universe, including all time and space.

In reality—In the highest realization of the Spirit there is no mind.

अहमेकमिदं सर्वं व्योमातीतं निरन्तरम् ।
पश्यामि कथमात्मानं प्रत्यक्षं वा तिरोहितम् ॥ १० ॥

aham ekam idaṁ sarvaṁ vyomātītaṁ nirantaram
paśyāmi katham ātmānaṁ pratyakṣaṁ vā tirohitam.

10. I, the One only, am all this, beyond space and continuous. How can I see the Self as visible or hidden?

Continuous—without the intervention of another substance; therefore homogeneous and undifferentiated.

Hidden—The question of the Self as being hidden or visible does not arise when one oneself is that Self.

त्वमेवमेकं हि कथं न बुध्यसे
समं हि सर्वेषु विमृष्टमव्ययम् ।
सदोदितोऽसि त्वमखण्डितः प्रभो
दिवा च नक्तं च कथं हि मन्यसे ॥ ११ ॥

tvam evam ekaṁ hi katham na buddhyase
samaṁ hi sarveṣu vimṛṣṭam avyayam
sadodito'si tvam akhanditaḥ prabho
divā ca naktaṁ ca kathaṁ hi manyase.

11. Thus you are One. Why then do you not understand that you are the unchangeable One, equally perceived in all? O mighty One, how can you, who are ever-shining, unrestricted, think of day and night?

You—Dattātreya now addresses the disciple to whom he is imparting the highest truth.

Night—There can be no perception of any time or condition in perfect Self-realization.

आत्मानं सततं विद्धि सर्वत्रैकं निरन्तरम् ।
अहं ध्याता परं ध्येयमखण्डं खण्ड्यते कथम् ॥ १२ ॥

ātmānaṁ satataṁ viddhi sarvatraikaṁ nirantaram
ahaṁ dhyātā paraṁ dhyeyam akhaṇḍaṁ khaṇḍyate katham.

12. Know the Self always to be everywhere, one and unintercepted. I am the meditator and

the highest object of meditation. Why do you divide the Indivisible?

Unintercepted—See note on "Continuous," verse 10.

Divide,etc.—Even the act of meditation is an expression of ignorance because it implies duality.

न जातो न मृतोऽसि त्वं न ते देहः कदाचन ।
सर्वं ब्रह्मेति विख्यातं ब्रवीति बहुधा श्रुतिः ॥ १३ ॥

na jāto na mṛto'si tvaṁ na te dehaḥ kadācana
sarvaṁ brahmeti vikhyātaṁ bravīti bahudhā śrutiḥ.

13. You are not born nor do you die. At no time do you have a body. The scripture declares in many different ways the well-known dictum: "All is Brahman."

स बाह्याभ्यन्तरोऽसि त्वं शिवः सर्वत्र सर्वदा ।
इतस्ततः कथं भ्रान्तः प्रधावसि पिशाचवत् ॥ १४ ॥

sa bāhyābhyantaro'si tvaṁ śivaḥ sarvatra sarvadā
itas tataḥ kathaṁ bhrāntaḥ pradhāvasi piśācavat.

14. You[1] are He who is exterior and interior. You are the auspicious One existing everywhere at all times. Why are you running hither and thither deluded, like an unclean spirit?

संयोगश्च वियोगश्च वर्तते न च ते न मे ।
न त्वं नाहं जगन्नेदं सर्वमात्मैव केवलम् ॥ १५ ॥

samyogaś ca viyogaś ca vartate na ca te na me
na tvaṁ nāhaṁ jagan-nedaṁ sarvam ātmaiva kevalam.

15. Union and separation exist in regard neither to you nor to me. There is no you, no me, nor is there this universe. All is verily the Self alone.

शब्दादिपञ्चकस्यास्य नैवासि त्वं न ते पुनः ।
त्वमेव परमं तत्त्वमतः किं परितप्यसे ॥ १६ ॥

śabdādi pañcakasyāsya naivāsi tvaṁ na te punaḥ
tvam eva paramam tattvam ataḥ kiṁ paritapyase.

16. You do not belong to that which is composed of the five objects of sense, such as sound; nor does that belong to you. You indeed are the supreme Reality. Why then do you suffer?

Five, etc.—The world appearance is composed of the five objects of sense: sight, sound, touch, taste, and smell, and is not in reality connected with the Self.

जन्म मृत्युर्न ते चित्तं बन्धमोक्षौ शुभाशुभौ ।
कथं रोदिषि रे वत्स नामरूपं न ते न मे ॥ १७ ॥

janma mṛtyuḥ na te cittaṁ bandha-mokṣau śubhāśubhau
kathaṁ rodisi re vatsa nāma-rūpaṁ na te na me.

17. For you there is no birth or death, for you there is no mind, for you there is no bondage or liberation, no good or evil. Why do you shed tears, my child? Neither you nor I have name and form.

अहो चित्त कथं भ्रान्तः प्रधावसि पिशाचवत् ।
अभिन्नं पश्य चात्मानं रागत्यागात्सुखी भव ।। १८ ।।

aho citta kathaṁ bhrāntaḥ pradhāvasi piśācavat
abhinnaṁ paśya cātmānaṁ rāga-tyāgāt sukhī bhava.

18. O mind, why do you wander about deluded, like an unclean spirit? Behold the Self indivisible. Be happy through renunciation of attachment.

त्वमेव तत्त्वं हि विकारवर्जितं
निष्कम्पमेकं हि विमोक्षविग्रहम् ।
न ते च रागो ह्यथवा विरागः
कथं हि सन्तप्यसि कामकामतः ।। १९ ।।

tvam eva tattvaṁ hi vikāra-varjitaṁ
niṣkampam ekaṁ hi vimokṣa-vigraham

na te ca rāgo hyathavā virāgah
katham hi santapyasi kāma-kāmataḥ.

19. You verily are Truth, devoid of change, motionless, one, of the nature of freedom. You have neither attachment nor aversion. Why do you suffer, seeking the objects of desires?

वदन्ति श्रुतयः सर्वाः निर्गुणं शुद्धमव्ययम् ।
अशरीरं समं तत्त्वं तन्मां विद्धि न संशयः ॥२०॥

vadanti śrutayah sarvāḥ nirgunam suddham avyayam
aśarīram samam tattvam tan mām viddhi na samśayaḥ

20. All the scriptures say that the Truth is without attributes, pure, immutable, bodiless, and existing equally everywhere. Know me to be That. There is not the least doubt about it.

साकारमनृतं विद्धि निराकारं निरन्तरम् ।
एतत्तत्त्वोपदेशेन न पुनर्भवसम्भवः ॥२१॥

sākāram anṛtam viddhi nirākāram nirantaram
etat tattvopadeśena na punar-bhava-sambhavaḥ.

21. Know that which has form to be false, that which is formless to be eternal. Through the

instruction of this truth there is no longer rebirth into this world.

No longer, etc.—Knowing oneself as eternal, one is not born into this world anymore, since incarnation is caused only by the soul's ignorance of its true nature.

एकमेव समं तत्त्वं वदन्ति हि विपश्चितः ।
रागत्यागात्पुनश्चित्तमेकानेकं न विद्यते ॥२२॥

ekam eva samaṁ tattvaṁ vadanti hi vipaścitaḥ
rāga-tyāgāt punaḥ cittam ekānekaṁ na vidyate.

22. Sages say that Reality is one only and the same. And through renunciation of attachment, the mind, which is one and many, ceases to exist.

One and many—"one" in a high (but not the highest) state of illumination, and "many" in the state of ignorance.

अनात्मरूपं च कथं समाधि-
रात्मस्वरूपं च कथं समाधिः ।
अस्तीति नास्तीति कथं समाधि-
र्मोक्षस्वरूपं यदि सर्वमेकम् ॥२३॥

anātma-rūpaṁ ca kathaṁ samādhiḥ
ātma-svarūpaṁ ca kathaṁ samādhiḥ
astīti nāstīti kathaṁ samādhiḥ
mokṣa-svarūpaṁ yadi sarvam ekam.

23. If it is of the nature of the not-Self, how can there be samādhi (superconscious realization)? If it is of the nature of the Self, how can there be samādhi? If it is both "is" and "is not", how can there be samādhi? If all is one and of the nature of freedom, how can there be samādhi?

It—the universe of experience.

Samādhi—the quieting and extinction of the mind, as a result of which the eternal Truth is realized. Dattātreya maintains that the practice of samādhi has no justification. If the universe of our experience is the not-Self, then we are not in the state of samādhi, for Truth is not there. If our experience is of the Self, then samādhi is superfluous.

विशुद्धोऽसि समं तत्त्वं विदेहस्त्वमजोऽव्ययः ।
जानामीह न जानामीत्यात्मानं मन्यसे कथम् ॥२४॥

viśuddho'si samaṁ tattvaṁ videhestvam ajo'vyayah
jānāmīha na jānāmity ātmānaṁ manyase katham.

24. You are pure homogeneous Reality, disembodied, unborn, and immutable. Why do you think of yourself as "I know it here" or as "I do not know"?

"I know it here", etc.—Our knowledge of ourself in this earthly state is incorrect. To maintain that we do not have any true knowledge of ourself here is also incorrect.

तत्त्वमस्यादिवाक्येन स्वात्मा हि प्रतिपादितः ।
नेति नेति श्रुतिर्ब्रूयादनृतं पाञ्चभौतिकम् ॥२५॥

tattvamasyādi vākyena svātmā hi pratipāditaḥ
neti neti śruṭir brūyāt anṛtaṁ pāñca-bhautikam.

25. By such sentences as "That thou art," your own Self is affirmed. Of that which is untrue and composed of the five elements the Sruti says, "Not this, not this."

That, etc.—the phenomenal existence.

Five elements—earth, water, fire, air, and ether, of which, according to the Indian systems of philosophy, the whole relative existence is constituted. See verse 3.

Śruti—the Vedas, particularly the Upaniṣads, the original texts of the Vedānta philosophy.

आत्मन्येवात्मना सर्वं त्वया पूर्णं निरन्तरम् ।
ध्याता ध्यानं न ते चित्तं निर्लज्जं
ध्यायते कथम् ॥२६॥

ātmany-evātmanā sarvaṁ tvayā pūrṇam
nirantaram
dhyātā dhyānaṁ na te cittaṁ nirlajjaṁ dhyāyate
katham.

26. As the self is filled by the Self, so is all filled continuously by you. There is no meditator or meditation. Why does your mind meditate shamelessly?

Shamelessly—One should be ashamed to meditate, because meditation presupposes a shameful forgetfulness of one's true, Divine nature.

शिवं न जानामि कथं वदामि
शिवं न जानामि कथं भजामि ।
अहं शिवश्चेत्परमार्थतत्त्वं
समस्वरूपं गगनोपमं च ॥ २७ ॥

śivaṁ na jānāmi kathaṁ vadāmi
śivaṁ na jānāmi kathaṁ bhajāmi
ahaṁ śivaś cet paramārtha-tattvaṁ
sama-svarūpaṁ gaganopamaṁ ca.

27. I do not know the Supreme; how shall I speak of Him? I do not know the Supreme; how shall I worship Him? If I am the supreme One, who is the highest Truth, who is homogeneous Being and like unto space, how then shall I speak of Him and worship Him?

Know, etc.—Empirical knowledge belongs to a lower state in which the Supreme cannot be perceived; therefore one cannot speak of "knowing" the Supreme.

नाहं तत्त्वं समं तत्त्वं कल्पनाहेतुवर्जितम् ।
ग्राह्यग्राहकनिर्मुक्तं स्वसंवेद्यं कथं भवेत् ॥ २८ ॥

nāhaṁ tattvaṁ samaṁ tattvaṁ kalpanā-hetu-varjitam
grāhya-grāhaka-nirmuktaṁ svasaṁvedyaṁ kathaṁ bhavet.

28. The principle of ego is not the Truth, which is homogeneous, which is free from the cause of superimposition and distinctions of perceived and perceiver. How can the ego be That which is aware of Itself?

अनन्तरूपं न हि वस्तु किञ्चि-
तत्त्वस्वरूपं न हि वस्तु किञ्चित् ।
आत्मैकरूपं परमार्थतत्त्वं
न हिंसको वापि न चाप्यहिंसा ॥ २९ ॥

ananta-rūpaṁ na hi vastu kiṁcit
tattva-svarūpaṁ na hi vastu kiṁcit
ātmaikarūpaṁ paramārtha-tattvaṁ
na hiṁsako vāpi nacāpy-ahiṁsā.

29. There is no substance whatever which is by nature unlimited. There is no substance whatever which is of the nature of Reality. The very Self is the supreme Truth. There is neither injury nor noninjury in It.

Substance—relative reality.

विशुद्धोऽसि समं तत्त्वं विदेहमजमव्ययम् ।
विभ्रमं कथमात्मार्थे विभ्रान्तोऽहं कथं पुनः ॥ ३० ॥

viśuddho'si samaṁ tattvaṁ videham-ajam-avyayam
vibhramaṁ katham ātmārthe vibhrānto'haṁ kathaṁ punaḥ.

30. You are the homogeneous Reality; you are pure, bodiless, birthless, and imperishable. Why then do you have any delusion about the Self? Again, why am I myself deluded?

घटे भिन्ने घटाकाशं सुलीनं भेदवर्जितम् ।
शिवेन मनसा शुद्धो न भेदः प्रतिभाति मे ॥ ३१ ॥

ghaṭe bhinne ghaṭākāśaṁ sulīnaṁ bheda-varjitam
śivena manasā śuddho na bhedaḥ pratibhāti me.

31. When the pot is broken, the space within it is absorbed in the infinite space and becomes undifferentiated. When the mind becomes pure, I do not perceive any difference between the mind and the supreme Being.

न घटो न घटाकाशो न जीवो जीवविग्रहः ।
केवलं ब्रह्म संविद्धि वेद्यवेदकवर्जितम् ॥ ३२ ॥

na ghaṭo na ghaṭākāśo na jīvo jīva-vigrahaḥ
kevalaṁ brahma samviddhi vedya-vedaka-
varjitam.

32 There is no pot; there is no pot's interior space. Neither is there an individual soul nor the form of an individual soul. Know the absolute Brahman, devoid of knowable and knower.

सर्वत्र सर्वदा सर्वमात्मानं सततं ध्रुवम् ।
सर्वं शून्यमशून्यं च तन्मां विद्धि न संशयः ॥ ३३ ॥

sarvatra sarvadā sarvam ātmānaṁ satataṁ
dhruvam
sarvaṁ śūnyam aśūnyaṁ ca tan māṁ viddhi
na saṁśayah.

33. Know me to be that Self who is everything and everywhere at all times, who is eternal, steady, the All, the nonexistent, and the Existent. Have no doubt.

Nonexistent—the phenomenal aspect of being, which has now disappeared.

वेदा न लोका न सुरा न यज्ञा वर्णाश्रमो नैव
कुलं न जातिः ।
न धूममार्गो न च दीप्तिमार्गो ब्रह्मैकरूपं
परमार्थतत्त्वम् ॥ ३४ ॥

vedāḥ na lokāḥ na surāḥ na yajñāḥ
varṇāśramo naiva kulaṁ na jātiḥ
na dhūma-mārgo na ca dīpti-mārgo
brahmaikarūpaṁ paramārtha-tattvam.

34. There are no Vedas, no worlds, no gods, no sacrifices. There is certainly no caste, no stage in life, no family, no birth. There is neither the path of smoke nor the path of light. There is only the highest Truth, the homogeneous Brahman.

Stage in life—any of the four stages into which life is divided by the Hindus, namely, those of the student, the householder, the contemplative, and the mendicant.

The path of smoke, etc.—the two paths along which, according to Hinduism, souls travel to the invisible worlds after death.

व्याप्यव्यापकनिर्मुक्तः त्वमेकः सफलं यदि ।
प्रत्यक्षं चापरोक्षं च ह्यात्मानं मन्यसे कथम् ॥३५॥

vyāpya-vyāpaka-nirmuktaḥ tvam ekaḥ
saphalaṁ yadi
pratyakṣaṁ cāparokṣaṁ ca hyātmānaṁ manyase
katham.

35. If you are free of the pervaded and pervader, if you are one and fulfilled, how can you

think of yourself as directly perceptible by the senses or beyond the range of the senses?

Free, etc.—one who has transcended the sense of distinction between forms ("pervaded") and the Divine Substance ("pervader"). Such a one, therefore, has constant, unobstructed consciousness of Divinity.

Directly—that is to say, in the manner in which the ignorant man perceives with his senses. In the highest state of realization, sense perception is no longer distinguishable from spiritual intuition.

अद्वैतं केचिदिच्छन्ति द्वैतमिच्छन्ति चापरे ।
समं तत्त्वं न विन्दन्ति द्वैताद्वैतविवर्जितम् ॥ ३६ ॥

advaitaṁ kecid icchanti dvaitam icchanti cāpare
samaṁ tattvaṁ na vindanti dvaitādvaita-vivarjitam.

36. Some seek nonduality, others duality. They do not know the Truth, which is the same at all times and everywhere, which is devoid of both duality and nonduality.

श्वेतादिवर्णरहितं शब्दादिगुणवर्जितम् ।
कथयन्ति कथं तत्त्वं मनोवाचामगोचरम् ॥ ३७ ॥

śvetādi-varṇa-rahitaṁ śabdādi-guṇa-varjitam
kathayanti kathaṁ tattvaṁ manovācām agocaram.

37. How can they describe the Truth, which is beyond mind and words, which is devoid of white and other colours, of sound and other qualities?

यदाऽनृतमिदं सर्वं देहादिगगनोपमम् ।
तदा हि ब्रह्म संवेत्ति न ते द्वैतपरम्परा ॥ ३८ ॥

yadā'nṛtam idaṁ sarvaṁ dehādi gaganopamam
tadā hi brahma saṁvetti na te dvaita-param-
parā.

38. When all these appear to you as false, when the body and so on appear to you like space, then you know Brahman truly, then for you there is no dual series.

Dual series—such as "I and Thou" (self and God), "I and it" (self and the world), and so on. Also it means "Self and not-Self" and the series of their evolutes.

परेण सहजात्मापि ह्यभिन्नः प्रतिभाति मे ।
व्योमाकारं तथैवैकं ध्याता ध्यानं कथं भवेत् ॥ ३९ ॥

pareṇa sahajātmāpi hya-bhinnaḥ pratibhāti me
vyomākāraṁ tathaivaikaṁ dhyātā dhyānaṁ
kathaṁ bhavet.

39. Even my natural self appears to me as non-distinct from the supreme Self; it appears to be

one and like space. How can there be meditator and meditation?

यत्करोमि यदश्नामि यज्जुहोमि ददामि यत् ।
एतत्सर्वं न मे किञ्चिद्विशुद्धोऽहमजोऽव्ययः ॥ ४० ॥

yat karomi yad aśnāmi yaj juhomi dadāmi yat
etat sarvaṁ na me kiñcit viśuddho'ham ajo'vyayaḥ

40. What I do, what I eat, what I sacrifice, what I give—all this is not mine in the least. I am pure, unborn, undecaying.

सर्वं जगद्विद्धि निराकृतीदं सर्वं जगद्विद्धि विकारहीनम् ।
सर्वं जगद्विद्धि विशुद्धदेहं सर्वं जगद्विद्धि शिवैकरूपम् ॥ ४१ ॥

sarvaṁ jagad viddhi nirākṛtīdaṁ
sarvaṁ jagad viddhi vikāra-hīnam
sarvaṁ jagad viddhi viśuddha-dehaṁ
sarvaṁ jagad viddhi śivaikarūpam.

41. Know all this universe to be formless. Know all this universe to be without change. Know all this universe to be of purified body. Know all this universe to be of the nature of the Absolute.

Of purified body—That is to say, the material substance of which the universe appears to be constituted is really nothing but pure Spirit.

तत्त्वं त्वं न हि संदेहः किं जानाम्यथवा पुनः ।
असंवेद्यं स्वसंवेद्यमात्मानं मन्यसे कथम् ॥ ४२ ॥

tattvaṁ tvaṁ na hi sandehaḥ kiṁ jānāmi athavā punaḥ
asaṁvedyaṁ svasaṁvedyam ātmānaṁ manyase katham.

42. You are verily the Truth. There is no doubt about it—otherwise, what do I know? Why do you consider the Self, which is perceptible to Itself, as imperceptible?

Otherwise—If one does not perceive every being as Divine, one is still ignorant.

मायाऽमाया कथं तात छायाऽछाया न विद्यते ।
तत्त्वमेकमिदं सर्वं व्योमाकारं निरञ्जनम् ॥ ४३ ॥

māyā amāyā kathaṁ tāta chāyā achāyā na vidyate
tattvam ekam idaṁ sarvaṁ vyomākāraṁ nirañjanam.

43. My child, how can there be illusion and nonillusion, shadow and lack of shadow? All

this is one Truth, all this is of the nature of space and without taint.

आदिमध्यान्तमुक्तोऽहं न बद्धोऽहं कदाचन ।
स्वभावनिर्मलः शुद्ध इति मे निश्चिता मतिः ॥ ४४ ॥

ādi-madhyānta-mukto'haṁ na baddho'haṁ kadācana
svabhāva-nirmalaḥ śuddhaḥ iti me niścitā matiḥ.

44. I am free in the beginning, in the middle, and in the end. I am never bound. This is my sure knowledge—that I am naturally spotless and pure.

महदादि जगत्सर्वं न किञ्चित्प्रतिभाति मे ।
ब्रह्मैव केवलं सर्वं कथं वर्णाश्रमस्थितिः ॥ ४५ ॥

mahad-ādi jagat sarvaṁ na kiñcit pratibhāti me
brahmaiva kevalaṁ sarvaṁ kathaṁ varṇā-śrama-sthitiḥ.

45. The whole universe, beginning with the principle of cosmic intelligence, is not in the least manifest to me. All is indeed Brahman alone. How can there be any existence in caste or stage of life for me?

जानामि सर्वथा सर्वमहमेको निरन्तरम् ।
निरालम्बमशून्यं च शून्यं व्योमादिपञ्चकम् ॥ ४६ ॥

jānāmi sarvathā sarvam aham eko nirantaram
nirālambam aśūnyaṁ ca śūnyaṁ vyomādi-
pañcakam.

46. I know that all, in every way, is the one indivisible "I" which is self-sustained and full, while the five elements, beginning with ether, are empty.

न षण्ढो न पुमान्न स्त्री न बोधो नैव कल्पना ।
सानन्दो वा निरानन्दमात्मानं मन्यसे कथम् ॥ ४७ ॥

na ṣaṇḍho na pumān na strī na bodho naiva
kalpanā
sānando vā nirānandam ātmanaṁ manyase
katham.

47. The Self is neither eunuch, man, nor woman: it is neither idea nor imagination. How can you think the Self to be full of joy or joyless?

Full of joy—Here "joy" is used in the sense of relative joy as perceived by the senses and the mind.

Joyless—Here the reference is to transcendental Joy.

षडङ्गयोगान्न तु नैव शुद्धं मनोविनाशान्न
तु नैव शुद्धम् ।
गुरूपदेशान्न तु नैव शुद्धं स्वयं च तत्त्वं
स्वयमेव बुद्धम् ॥४८॥

ṣaḍaṅga yogān na tu naiva śuddhaṁ
mano-vināśān na tu naiva śuddham
gurūpadeśān na tu naiva śuddhaṁ
svayaṁ ca tattvaṁ svayam eva buddham.

48. The Self certainly does not become pure through the practice of six-limbed yoga. It certainly is not purified by the destruction of the mind. It certainly is not made pure by the instructions of the teacher. It is Itself the Truth, It is Itself the illumined One.

Six-limbed—consisting of six parts or steps, namely, posture, control of the vital force, self-withdrawal, concentration, meditation, and samādhi.

न हि पञ्चात्मको देहो विदेहो वर्तते न हि ।
आत्मैव केवलं सर्वं तुरीयं च त्रयं कथम् ॥४९॥

na hi pañcātmako deho videho vartate na hi
ātmaiva kevalaṁ sarvaṁ turīyaṁ ca trayaṁ
katham.

49. There is no body made up of five elements; nor is there anyone who is disembodied. All is

verily the Self alone. How can there be the three states and the fourth?

Five elements—See verses 3 and 25.

Anyone, etc.—When the pure Self is spoken of as disembodied, the idea of body is associated with It, though negatively. All such qualifications of the Self (or Soul) are denied in this as well as in other verses.

Three states, etc.—the waking state, the dream state, and the deep sleep state: the ordinary conditions of individuals when they are ignorant of their true nature, which is usually called the fourth or transcendental state. To name the transcendental state as the fourth is itself an error, as such a designation, which makes it a correlative of the other three states, is inapplicable to the absolute Self.

न बद्धो नैवमुक्तोऽहं न चाहं ब्रह्मणः पृथक् ।
न कर्ता न च भोक्ताहं व्याप्यव्यापकवर्जितः ॥ ५० ॥

na baddho naiva mukto'haṁ na cāhaṁ brahmaṇaḥ pṛthak
na kartā na ca bhoktāhaṁ vyāpya-vyāpaka-varjitaḥ.

50. I am not bound, I am not, indeed, liberated, and I am not different from Brahman. Neither doer nor enjoyer, I am devoid of the distinctions of the pervaded and the pervader.

Liberated—The Self cannot be "liberated", since it was never bound.

Pervaded, etc.—The Sanskrit words for pervaded and pervader are vyāpya and vyāpaka, meaning the particular and the universal. The particular is pervaded by or constituted of the universal. The Self can be neither particular nor universal, as both these designations imply distinction, division, and limitation.

यथा जलं जले न्यस्तं सलिलं भेदवर्जितम् ।
प्रकृतिं पुरुषं तद्वदभिन्नं प्रतिभाति मे ॥ ५१ ॥

yathā jalaṁ jale nyastaṁ salilaṁ bheda-varjitam
prakṛtiṁ puruṣaṁ tadvad abhinnaṁ pratibhāti me.

51. As water, when water has been poured into water, has no distinctions, so purusa and prakṛti appear nondifferent to me.

Purusa, etc.—puruṣa: Soul. prakṛti: nature. Ordinarily considered to be opposite principles, conscious and unconscious, they are here recognized as identical in the highest spiritual experience.

यदि नाम न मुक्तोऽसि न बद्धोऽसि कदाचन ।
साकारं च निराकारमात्मानं मन्यसे कथम् ॥ ५२ ॥

yadi nāma na mukto'si na baddho'si kadācana
sākāraṁ ca nirākāram atmānaṁ manyase katham?

52. If indeed you are never bound or liberated, how then can you think yourself with form or as formless?

With form,etc.—The Self, of course, is without form, but saying so implies recognition of form; therefore even the idea of the formlessness of the Self is repudiated.

जानामि ते परं रूपं प्रत्यक्षं गगनोपमम् ।
यथा परं हि रूपं यन्मरीचिजलसन्निभम् ॥ ५३ ॥

jānāmi te paraṁ rūpaṁ pratyakṣaṁ gaganopamam
yathā paraṁ hi rūpaṁ yan marīci-jala-sannibham.

53. I know your supreme Form to be directly perceivable, like the sky. I know your lower form to be as water in a mirage.

Like the sky—without division or distinction, without change.

Lower, etc.—apparent form.

न गुरुर्नोपदेशश्च न चोपाधिर्न मे क्रिया ।
विदेहं गगनं विद्धि विशुद्धोऽहं स्वभावतः ॥ ५४ ॥

na guruḥ nopadeśaś ca na copādhir na me kriyā
videhaṁ gaganaṁ viddhi viśuddho'haṁ svabhā-
vataḥ.

54. I have neither teacher nor instruction, limiting adjunct nor activity. Know that I am by nature pure, bodiless, like the sky.

Limiting, etc.—any qualification.

विशुद्धोऽस्य शरीरोऽसि न ते चित्तं परात्परम् ।
अहं चात्मा परं तत्त्वमिति वक्तुं न लज्जसे ॥ ५५ ॥

viśuddho'sya śarīro'si na te cittaṁ parāt param
ahaṁ cātmā paraṁ tattvam iti vaktuṁ na
lajjase.

55. You are pure, you are without a body, your mind is not higher than the highest. You need not be ashamed to say, "I am the Self, the supreme Truth."

Mind, etc.—The mind is not the Self.

कथं रोदिषि रे चित्त ह्यात्मैवात्मात्मना भव ।
पिब वत्स कलातीतमद्वैतं परमामृतम् ॥ ५६ ॥

kathaṁ rodiṣi re citta hy ātmaivātmātmanā
bhava
piba vatsa kalātītam advaitaṁ paramāmṛtam.

56. Why are you weeping, O mind? Do you, the Self, be the Self by means of the Self. Drink, my child, the supreme nectar of Nonduality, transcending all divisions.

Means,etc.—One cannot attain to Self-knowledge except through the Self itself. How can the mind, which is not-Self, reveal the Self?

नैव बोधो न चाबोधो न बोधाबोध एव च ।
यस्येदृशः सदा बोधः स बोधो नान्यथा भवेत् ॥ ५७॥

naiva bodho na cābodho na bodhābodha eva ca
yasyedṛśaḥ sadā bodhaḥ sa bodho nānyathā bhavet.

57. There is neither knowledge nor ignorance nor knowledge combined with ignorance. He who has always such knowledge is himself Knowledge. It is never otherwise.

Knowledge—The Absolute is spoken of as Existence, Knowledge, and Bliss.

ज्ञानं न तर्को न समाधियोगो न देशकालौ न गुरूपदेशः ।
स्वभावसंवित्तिरहं च तत्त्वमाकाशकल्पं सहजं ध्रुवं च ॥ ५८ ॥

jñānaṁ na tarko na samādhi yogo
na deśa-kālau na gurūpadeśaḥ
svabhāva-saṁvittir ahaṁ ca tattvaṁ
ākāśa-kalpaṁ sahajaṁ dhruvaṁ ca.

58. There is no need of knowledge, reasoning, time, space, instruction from a teacher, or attainment of samādhi. I am naturally the perfect Consciousness, the Real, like the sky, spontaneous and steady.

Samādhi—See verse 23. Dattātreya maintains that the practice of samādhi is not necessary because, according to him, the Self has never been bound and hence does not require to practise anything to gain knowledge of Itself. The Self, which is Consciousness Itself, can never lose consciousness of Its true nature and therefore samādhi is superfluous.

न जातोऽहं मृतो वापि न मे कर्म शुभाशुभम् ।
विशुद्धं निर्गुणं ब्रह्म बन्धो मुक्तिः कथं मम ॥ ५९ ॥

na jāto'haṁ mṛto vāpi na me karma śubhāśubham
viśuddhaṁ nirguṇaṁ brahma bandho muktiḥ kathaṁ mama.

59. I was not born nor have I death. I have no action, good or evil. I am Brahman, stainless, without qualities. How can there be bondage or liberation for me?

यदि सर्वंगतो देवः स्थिरः पूर्णो निरन्तरः ।
अन्तरं हि न पश्यामि स बाह्याभ्यन्तरः
कथम् ॥ ६० ॥

yadi sarva-gato devaḥ sthiraḥ pūrṇaḥ nirantaraḥ
antaraṁ hi na paśyāmi sa bāhyābhyantaraḥ
katham.

60. If God pervades all, if God is immovable, full, undivided, then I see no division. How can He have exterior or interior?

How, etc.—Exterior or interior cannot be spoken of Him who is indivisible and infinite.

स्फुरत्येव जगत्कृत्स्नमखण्डितनिरन्तरम् ।
अहो मायामहामोहो द्वैताद्वैतविकल्पना ॥ ६१ ॥

sphuratyeva jagat kṛtsnam akhaṇḍita-nirantaram
aho māyā mahā-moho dvaitādvaita-vikalpanā.

61. The whole universe shines undivided and unbroken. Oh, the māyā, the great delusion—the imagination of duality and nonduality!

Māyā—ignorance.

साकारं च निराकारं नेति नेतीति सर्वदा ।
भेदाभेदविनिर्मुक्तो वर्तते केवलः शिवः ॥ ६२ ॥

sākāraṁ ca nirākāraṁ neti netīti sarvadā
bhedābheda-vinirmukto vartate kevalaḥ śivaḥ.

62. Always "not this, not this" to both the formless and the formed. Only the Absolute exists, transcending difference and nondifference.

"Not this", etc.—No formed or formless object can be considered to be the ultimate Reality.

न ते च माता च पिता च बन्धुः
न ते च पत्नी न सुतश्च मित्रम् ।
न पक्षपातो न विपक्षपातः
कथं हि संतप्तिरियं हि चित्ते ॥ ६३ ॥

na te ca mātā ca pitā ca bandhuḥ
na te ca patnī na sutaś ca mitram
na pakṣapāto na vipakṣapātaḥ
kathaṁ hi santaptir iyaṁ hi citte.

63. You have no mother, no father, no wife, no son, no relative, no friend. You have no likes or dislikes. Why is this anguish in your mind?

दिवा नक्तं न ते चित्तं उदयास्तमयौ न हि ।
विदेहस्य शरीरत्वं कल्पयन्ति कथं बुधाः ॥ ६४॥

divā naktaṁ na te cittam udayāstamayau na hi
videhasya śarīratvaṁ kalpayanti kathaṁ budhāḥ.

64. O mind, for you there is no day or night, rising or setting. How can the wise imagine an embodied state for the bodiless?

नाविभक्तं विभक्तं च न हि दुःखसुखादि च ।
न हि सर्वमसर्वं च विद्धि चात्मानमव्ययम् ॥ ६५ ॥

nāvibhaktaṁ vibhaktaṁ ca nahi duḥkha-sukhādi ca
na hi sarvam asarvaṁ ca viddhi cātmānam avyayam.

65. The Self is neither divided nor undivided, nor has It sadness, happiness, and the like, nor is It all or less than all. Know the Self to be immutable.

नाहं कर्ता न भोक्ता च न मे कर्म पुराऽधुना ।
न मे देहो विदेहो वा निर्ममेति ममेति किम् ॥ ६६ ॥

nāhaṁ kartā na bhoktā ca na me karma purā-'dhunā
na me deho videho vā nirmameti mameti kim.

66. I am not the doer or enjoyer. Work have I none, now or formerly. I have no body,

nor am I bodiless. How can I have or not have a sense of "my-ness"?

न मे रागादिको दोषो दुःखं देहादिकं न मे ।
आत्मानं विद्धि मामेकं विशालं गगनोपमम् ॥ ६७ ॥

na me rāgādiko doṣo duḥkhaṁ dehādikaṁ na me
ātmānaṁ viddhi mām ekaṁ viśālaṁ gagano-pamam.

67. I have no fault such as passion and the like, nor have I any sorrow arising from the body. Know me to be the one Self, vast and like the sky.

सखे मनः किं बहुजल्पितेन
सखे मनः सर्वमिदं वितर्क्यम् ।
यत्सारभूतं कथितं मया ते
त्वमेव तत्त्वं गगनोपमोऽसि ॥ ६८ ॥

sakhe manaḥ kiṁ bahu jalpitena
sakhe manaḥ sarvam idaṁ vitarkyam
yat sāra-bhūtaṁ kathitaṁ mayā te
tvam eva tattvaṁ gaganopamo'si.

68. Friend mind, of what use is much vain talk? Friend mind, all this is mere conjecture. I have told you that which is the essence: you indeed are the Truth, like the sky.

All, etc.—Words and ideas, being finite and related to finite objects, can never reveal Truth completely.

येन केनापि भावेन यत्र कुत्र मृता अपि ।
योगिनस्तत्र लीयन्ते घटाकाशमिवांबरे ॥ ६९ ॥

yena kenāpi bhāvena yatra kutra mṛtā api
yoginaḥ tatra līyante ghaṭākāśam ivāṁbare.

69. In whatever place yogīs die, in whatever state, there they dissolve, as the space of a jar dissolves into the sky.

Dissolve, etc.—become identified with the Self.

तीर्थे चान्त्यजगेहे वा नष्टस्मृतिरपि त्यजन् ।
समकाले तनुं मुक्तः कैवल्यव्यापको भवेत् ॥ ७० ॥

tirthe cāntyaja-gehe vā naṣṭa-smṛtir api tyajan
sama-kāle tanuṁ muktaḥ kaivalya-vyāpako bhavet.

70. Giving up the body in a holy place or in the house of a caṇḍāla, the yogī, even if he has lost consciousness, becomes identified with the Absolute as soon as he is free of the body.

Caṇḍāla—one belonging to the lowest stratum—considered unclean and impure—of Hindu society.

Lost, etc.—that is to say, apparently so. The inward awareness of the yogī can never be clouded.

धर्मार्थकाममोक्षांश्च द्विपदादिचराचरम् ।
मन्यन्ते योगिनः सर्वं मरीचिजलसन्निभम् ॥ ७१ ॥

dharmārtha-kāma-mokṣāṁśca dvipadādi-carācaram
manyante yoginaḥ sarvaṁ marīci-jala-sannibham.

71. The yogīs consider duty in life, pursuit of wealth, enjoyment of love, liberation, and everything movable or immovable such as man and so on to be a mirage.

अतीतानागतं कर्म वर्तमानं तथैव च ।
न करोमि न भुञ्जामि इति मे निश्चला मतिः ॥७२॥

atītānāgataṁ karma vartamānaṁ tathaiva ca
na karomi na bhuñjāmi iti me niścalā matiḥ.

72. This is my certain perception: I neither perform nor enjoy past action, future action, or present action.

शून्यागारे समरसपूत-
स्तिष्ठन्नेकः सुखमवधूतः ।
चरति हि नग्नस्त्यक्त्वा गर्वं
विन्दति केवलमात्मनि सर्वम् ॥ ७३ ॥

śūnyāgāre samarasa-pūtaḥ
tiṣṭhannekaḥ sukham avadhūtaḥ
carati hi nagnaḥ tyaktvā garvaṁ
vindati kevalam ātmani sarvam.

73. The avadhūta, alone, pure in evenness of feeling, abides happy in an empty dwelling place. Having renounced all, he moves about naked. He perceives the Absolute, the All, within himself.

Avadhūta—a liberated soul, one who has "passed away from" or "shaken off" all worldly attachments and cares, and has realized his identity with God.

त्रितयतुरीयं नहि नहि यत्र
विन्दति केवलमात्मनि तत्र ।
धर्माधर्मौ नहि नहि यत्र
बद्धो मुक्तः कथमिह तत्र ॥ ७४ ॥

tritaya turīyaṁ nahi nahi yatra
vindati kevalam ātmani tatra
dharmādharmau nahi nahi yatra
baddho muktaḥ katham iha tatra.

74. Where there are neither the three states of consciousness nor the fourth, there one attains the Absolute in the Self. How is it possible to be bound or free where there is neither virtue nor vice?

विन्दति विन्दति नहि नहि मन्त्रं
छन्दोलक्षणं नहि नहि तन्त्रम् ।
समरसमग्नो भावितपूतः
प्रलपितमेतत्परमवधूतः ॥ ७५ ॥

vindati vindati nahi nahi mantraṁ
chando-lakṣaṇaṁ nahi nahi tantram
samarasa-magno bhāvita-pūtaḥ
pralapitam etat param avadhūtaḥ.

75. The avadhūta never knows any mantra in Vedic metre nor any tantra. This is the supreme utterance of the avadhūta, purified by meditation and merged in the sameness of infinite Being.

Mantra—a hymn or a sacred prayer.

Tantra—system of rites and ceremonies.

This—the truth as enunciated in the whole discourse.

सर्वशून्यमशून्यं च सत्यासत्यं न विद्यते ।
स्वभावभावतः प्रोक्तं शास्त्रसंवित्तिपूर्वकम् ॥ ७६ ॥

sarva-śūnyam aśūnyaṁ ca satyāsatyaṁ na vidyate
svabhāva-bhāvataḥ proktaṁ śāstra-saṁvitti-pūrvakam.

76. There exists neither complete void nor voidlessness, neither truth nor untruth. The avadhūta, having realized the truths of the scriptures, has uttered this spontaneously from his own nature.

Truth—Complete Truth does not exist in the plane of relative existence.

Chapter II

बालस्य वा विषयभोगरतस्य वापि
मूर्खस्य सेवकजनस्य गृहस्थितस्य ।
एतद्गुरोः किमपि नैव न चिन्तनीयं
रत्नं कथं त्यजति कोऽप्यशुचौ प्रविष्टम् ॥ १ ॥

bālasya vā viṣaya-bhoga-ratasya vāpi
mūrkhasya sevaka-janasya gṛha-sthitasya
etad-guroḥ kim api naiva na cintanīyaṁ
ratnaṁ kathaṁ tyajati ko'pyaśucau praviṣṭam.

1. Of the teacher—even if he be young, illiterate, or addicted to the enjoyment of sense objects, even if he be a servant or a householder—none of these should be considered. Does anyone shun a gem fallen in an impure place?

Illiterate—not versed in the scriptures.

Addicted, etc.—apparently so.

नैवात्र काव्यगुण एव तु चिन्तनीयो
ग्राह्यः परं गुणवता खलु सार एव ।
सिन्दूरचित्ररहिता भुवि रूपशून्या
पारं न किं नयति नौरिह गन्तुकामान् ॥ २ ॥

naivātra kāvya-guṇa eva tu cintanīyo
grāhyaḥ paraṁ guṇavatā khalu sāra eva
sindūra-citra-rahitā bhuvi rūpa-śūnyā
pāraṁ na kiṁ nayati naur iha gantu-kāmān.

2. In such a case one should not consider even the quality of scholarship. A worthy person should recognize only the essence. Does not a boat, though devoid of beauty and vermilion paint, nevertheless ferry passengers?

Even,etc.—The essential qualification of the teacher is not intellectual eminence, but capacity to impart spiritual illumination.

प्रयत्नेन विना येन निश्चलेन चलाचलम् ।
ग्रस्तं स्वभावतः शान्तं चैतन्यं गगनोपमम् ॥ ३ ॥

prayatnena vinā yena niścalena calācalam
grastaṁ svabhāvataḥ śāntaṁ caitanyaṁ gaganopamam.

3. The unmoving One, who without effort possesses all that is movable and immovable, is Consciousness, naturally calm, like the sky.

अयत्नाच्चालयेद्यस्तु एकमेव चराचरम् ।
सर्वगं तत्कथं भिन्नमद्वैतं वर्तते मम ॥ ४ ॥

ayatnāc-cālayed yas-tu ekam eva carācaram
sarvagaṁ tat kathaṁ bhinnam advaitaṁ vartate mama.

4. How can He, the One and All-pervading, who moves effortlessly all that is movable and immovable, be differentiated! To me He is nondual.

अहमेव परं यस्मात्सारात्सारतरं शिवम् ।
गमागमविनिर्मुक्तं निर्विकल्पं निराकुलम् ॥ ५ ॥

aham eva paraṁ yasmāt sārātsārataraṁ śivam
gamāgama-vinirmuktaṁ nirvikalpaṁ nirākulam.

5. I am verily supreme since I am the Absolute, more essential than all essences, since I am free from birth and death, calm and undifferentiated.

सर्वावयवनिर्मुक्तं तथाहं त्रिदशार्चितम् ।
सम्पूर्णत्वान्न गृह्णामि विभागं त्रिदशादिकम् ॥ ६ ॥

sarvāvayava-nirmuktaṁ tathāhaṁ tridaśārcitam
saṁpūrṇatvān-na gṛhṇāmi vibhāgaṁ tridaśādikam.

6. Thus I, free from all components, am worshipped by the gods, but being full and

perfect, I do not recognize any distinctions such as gods and the like.

Free, etc.—not made up of parts; indivisible.

Worshipped, etc.—because the true Self is the highest Divinity.

Recognize, etc.—In the highest spiritual realization no distinctions and differences are perceived.

प्रमादेन न सन्देहः किं करिष्यामि वृत्तिमान् ।
उत्पद्यन्ते विलीयन्ते बुद्बुदाश्च यथा जले ॥ ७ ॥

pramādena na sandehaḥ kiṁ kariṣyāmi vṛttimān
utpadyante vilīyante budbudāś ca yathā jale.

7. Ignorance does not create any doubt. What shall I do, being endowed with modifications of the mind? They arise and dissolve like bubbles in water.

Ignorance, etc.—The man of the highest spiritual perception, after realizing his Divine identity, may live on the relative plane and thus appear enveloped by ignorance, but even then he is never unaware of his Divinity.

What, etc.—Though the man of highest spiritual perception appears to think, will, etc., yet, as the pure witness, he remains completely separate from mental activities.

महदादीनि भूतानि समाप्यैवं सदैव हि ।
मृदुद्रव्येषु तीक्ष्णेषु गुडेषु कटुकेषु च ॥ ८ ॥

mahadādīni bhūtāni samāpyaivaṁ sadaiva hi
mṛdudravyeṣu tīkṣṇeṣu guḍeṣu kaṭukeṣu ca.

8. Thus am I ever pervading all existence beginning with cosmic intelligence—pervading soft, hard, sweet, and pungent substances.

कटुत्वं चैव शैत्यत्वं मृदुत्वं च यथा जले ।
प्रकृतिः पुरुषस्तद्वदभिन्नं प्रतिभाति मे ॥ ९ ॥

kaṭutvaṁ caiva śaityatvaṁ mṛdutvaṁ ca yathā jale
prakṛtiḥ puruṣaḥ tadvat abhinnaṁ pratibhāti me.

9. As pungency, coldness, or softness is nondifferent from water, so prakṛti is nondifferent from puruṣa—thus it appears to me.

Prakṛti—nature; relative existence.

Puruṣa—spirit, the Absolute.

सर्वाख्यारहितं यद्यत्सूक्ष्मात्सूक्ष्मतरं परम् ।
मनोबुद्धीन्द्रियातीतमकलङ्कं जगत्पतिम् ॥ १० ॥

sarvākhyā-rahitaṁ yad yat sūkṣmāt sūkṣmataraṁ param
manobuddhīndriyātītam akalaṅkaṁ jagatpatim.

10. The Lord of the universe is devoid of all names. He is subtler than the subtlest, su-

preme. He is spotless, beyond the senses, mind, and intellect.

Lord, etc.—the Self.

ईदृशं सहजं यत्र अहं तत्र कथं भवेत् ।
त्वमेव हि कथं तत्र कथं तत्र चराचरम् ॥ ११ ॥

īdṛśaṁ sahajaṁ yatra ahaṁ tatra kathaṁ bhavet
tvameva hi kathaṁ tatra kathaṁ tatra carācaram.

11. Where there is such a natural Being, how can there be "I", how can there be even "you", how can there be the world?

Natural—existing in its natural (i.e., pure) state.

गगनोपमं तु यत्प्रोक्तं तदेव गगनोपमम् ।
चैतन्यं दोषहीनं च सर्वज्ञं पूर्णमेव च ॥ १२ ॥

gaganopamaṁ tu yat proktaṁ tad eva gaganopamam
caitanyaṁ doṣa-hīnaṁ ca sarvajñaṁ pūrṇam eva ca.

12. That which has been described as being like ether is indeed like ether. That is Consciousness—blameless, omniscient, and perfect.

पृथिव्यां चरितं नैव मारुतेन च वाहितम् ।
वारिणा पिहितं नैव तेजोमध्ये व्यवस्थितम् ॥ १३ ॥

pṛthivyāṁ caritaṁ naiva mārutena ca vāhitam
vāriṇā pihitaṁ naiva tejo-madhye vyavasthitam.

13. It does not move about on the earth or dwell in fire. It is not blown by the wind or covered by water.

आकाशं तेन संव्याप्तं न तद्व्याप्तं च केनचित् ।
स बाह्याभ्यन्तरं तिष्ठत्यवच्छिन्नं निरन्तरम् ॥ १४ ॥

ākāśaṁ tena saṁvyāptaṁ na tad vyāptaṁ ca kenacit
sa bāhyābhyantaraṁ tiṣṭhatyavacchinnaṁ nirantaram.

14. Space is pervaded by It, but It is not pervaded by anything. It is existing within and without. It is undivided and continuous.

सूक्ष्मत्वात्तददृश्यत्वान्निर्गुणत्वाच्च योगिभिः ।
आलम्बनादि यत्प्रोक्तं क्रमादालम्बनं भवेत् ॥ १५ ॥

sūkṣmatvāt tad adṛśyatvāt nirguṇatvāc ca yogibhiḥ
ālambanādi yat proktaṁ kramād ālambanaṁ bhavet.

15. One should successively take recourse to the objects of concentration, as mentioned by the yogīs, in accordance with their subtlety, invisibility, and attributelessness.

Take, etc.—In order to attain to the Absolute (or dissolution in the Absolute, as is said in the next verse), one has to reach the state of infinite and undifferentiated Consciousness by eliminating all mental differentiations or movements. The method of this elimination is to make consciousness dwell on one object continuously by obstructing its restless tendency to dwell on multifarious objects. But the object of concentration has to be chosen carefully. The beginner chooses a gross object. When he has dwelt on it continuously for some time, his consciousness becomes subtle and steady. He then chooses a subtle object to concentrate on. Gradually he reaches a high state of concentration, but some differentiations in his consciousness still remain—there is the consciousness of himself as the concentrator, of the object on which he is concentrating, and of the process of concentration. Next even these differentiations vanish. for the object of concentration dissolves, and there remains only the pure, undifferentiated Consciousness, the Absolute.

सतताऽभ्यासयुक्तस्तु निरालम्बो यदा भवेत् ।
तल्लयाल्लीयते नान्तर्गुणदोषविवर्जितः ॥ १६ ॥

satatā'bhyāsa-yuktas tu nirālaṁbo yadā bhavet
tal-layāt līyate nāntarguṇadoṣa-vivarjitaḥ.

16. When through constant practice one's concentration becomes objectless, then, being divested of merits and demerits, one attains the state of complete dissolution in the Absolute

through the dissolution of the object of concentration, but not before then.

विषविश्वस्य रौद्रस्य मोहमूर्च्छाप्रदस्य च ।
एकमेव विनाशाय ह्यमोघं सहजामृतम् ॥ १७ ॥

viṣa-viśvasya raudrasya moha-mūrcchā-pradasya ca
ekam eva vināśāya hi amoghaṁ sahajāmṛtam.

17. For the destruction of the terrible, poisonous universe, which produces the unconsciousness of delusion, there is but one infallible remedy—the nectar of naturalness.

Unconsciousness, etc.—delusion which makes one unconscious of the Divine Reality.

Naturalness—the state of pure Existence; Divine Identity.

भावगम्यं निराकारं साकारं दृष्टिगोचरम् ।
भावाभावविनिर्मुक्तमन्तरालं तदुच्यते ॥ १८ ॥

bhāva-gamyaṁ nirākāraṁ sākāraṁ dṛṣṭi-gocaram
bhāvābhāva-vinirmuktam antarālaṁ tad ucyate.

18. That which has form is visible to the eye, while the formless is perceived mentally. That (the Self), being beyond existence and nonexistence, is called intermediate.

Intermediate–neither material nor mental, i.e., beyond both.

बाह्यभावं भवेद्विश्वमन्तः प्रकृतिरुच्यते ।
अन्तरादन्तरं ज्ञेयं नारिकेलफलाम्बुवत् ॥ १९ ॥

bāhya-bhāvaṁ bhaved viśvam antaḥ prakṛtir ucyate
antarādantaraṁ jñeyaṁ nārikela-phalāmbuvat.

19. The external existence is the universe, the inner existence is called prakṛti. One should try to know That which is more interior than the inner existence, That which is like water within the kernel of the coconut.

Prakṛti—in its subtle aspects: cosmic intelligence, cosmic mind, etc.

भ्रान्तिज्ञानं स्थितं बाह्यं सम्यग्ज्ञानं च मध्यगम् ।
मध्यान्मध्यतरं ज्ञेयं नारिकेलफलाम्बुवत् ॥ २० ॥

bhrānti-jñānaṁ sthitaṁ bāhyaṁ samyag jñānaṁ ca madhyagam
madhyān madhyataraṁ jñeyaṁ nārikela-phalāmbuvat.

20. Illusory knowledge relates to what is outside, correct knowledge to what is inside. Try to know That which is more interior than the

inside, That which is like water within the kernel of the coconut.

पौर्णमास्यां यथा चन्द्र एक एवातिनिर्मलः ।
तेन तत्सदृशं पश्येद्द्विधादृष्टिर्विपर्ययः ॥ २१ ॥

paurṇamāsyāṁ yathā candra eka evātinirmalaḥ
tena tat-sadṛśaṁ paśyet dvidhā-dṛṣṭiḥ viparyayaḥ.

21. There is only one very clear moon on the full moon night. One should perceive That (the Self) like the moon; seeing duality is perversion.

अनेनैव प्रकारेण बुद्धिभेदो न सर्वगः ।
दाता च धीरतामेति गीयते नामकोटिभिः ॥ २२ ॥

anenaiva prakāreṇa buddhi-bhedo na sarvagaḥ
dātā ca dhīratām eti gīyate nāma-koṭibhiḥ.

22. It is indeed in this way that intelligence becomes divided and ceases to be all-comprehending. A giver attains to wisdom and is sung with millions of names.

This,etc.—by seeing duality (also, of course, plurality).

Divided—perceiving many objects separated from one another, as in ordinary experience. Intelligence should, if it is not clouded with ignorance, perceive only unity—the whole of Reality—at once. Such perception, according to Vedānta, is the only true perception of Reality.

Giver—maker of charity. The second part of this verse, and, as a matter of fact, the whole verse, is a little obscure. Our translation of the second part is literal. The probable meaning is: When a person gives away all he possesses in charity and thereby attains to perfect renunciation, being free of all worldliness he attains to the knowledge of the Self and is praised in various ways for both his charity and his spiritual knowledge. The Sanskrit *dātā* for the word "giver" also means a teacher.

गुरुप्रज्ञाप्रसादेन मूर्खो वा यदि पण्डितः ।
यस्तु संबुध्यते तत्त्वं विरक्तो भवसागरात् ॥ २३ ॥

guru-prajñāprasādena murkho vā yadi paṇḍitaḥ
yastu sambudhyate tattvaṁ virakto bhava-sāgarāt.

23. Whoever, whether he be ignorant or learned, attains to the full awareness of Truth through the grace of a teacher's wisdom, becomes detached from the ocean of worldliness.

Ignorant—devoid of scholarship.

रागद्वेषविनिर्मुक्तः सर्वभूतहिते रतः ।
दृढबोधश्च धीरश्च स गच्छेत्परमं पदम् ॥ २४ ॥

rāgadveṣa-vinırmuktaḥ sarvabhūta-hite rataḥ
dṛḍha-bodhaś ca dhīraś ca sa gacchet paramaṁ padam.

24. He who is free from attachment and hatred, devoted to the good of all beings, fixed in knowledge and steady shall attain to the supreme state.

घटे भिन्ने घटाकाश आकाशे लीयते यथा ।
देहाभावे तथा योगी स्वरूपे परमात्मनि ॥ २५ ॥

ghaṭe bhinne ghaṭākāśa ākāśe līyate yathā
dehābhāve tathā yogī svarūpe paramātmani.

25. As the space within a pot dissolves in the universal space when the pot is broken, so a yogī, in the absence of the body, dissolves into the supreme Self, which is his true being.

उक्तेयं कर्मयुक्तानां मतिर्यान्तेऽपि सा गतिः ।
न चोक्ता योगयुक्तानां मतिर्यान्तेऽपि सा गतिः ॥ २६ ॥

ukteyaṁ karma-yuktānāṁ matir yānte'pi sā gatiḥ
na coktā yoga-yuktānāṁ matir yānte'pi sā gatiḥ.

26. It has been said that the destiny of those devoted to action is the same as their thought

at the end, but it has not been said that the destiny of those established in yoga is the same as their thought at the end.

End—the dying moment. The belief in India, clearly expressed in the *Bhagavad Gītā*, is that the last thought in the mind of the dying person indicates the nature of his future existence. This is not true, however, of one who has attained to the knowledge of the Self.

या गतिः कर्मयुक्तानां सा च वागिन्द्रियाद्वदेत् ।
योगिनां या गतिः क्वापि ह्यकथ्या
भवतोर्जिता ॥ २७ ॥

yā gatiḥ karma-yuktānāṁ sā ca
vāgindriyād vadet
yogināṁ yā gatiḥ kvāpi hy akathyā bhavatorjitā.

27. One may express the destiny of those devoted to action with the organ of speech, but the destiny of the yogīs can never be expressed, because it is transcendental.

एवं ज्ञात्वा त्वमुं मार्गं योगिनां नैव कल्पितम् ।
विकल्पवर्जनं तेषां स्वयं सिद्धिः प्रवर्तते ॥ २८ ॥

evaṁ jñātvā tvamuṁ mārgaṁ yogināṁ naiva
kalpitam
vikalpa-varjanaṁ teṣāṁ svayaṁ siddhiḥ
pravartate.

28. Knowing this, one never says that the yogīs have any particular path. For them it is the giving up of all duality. The supreme attainment comes of itself.

Particular, etc.—Departing souls reach their destined worlds following either pitṛ-yāna, the path of the fathers, or deva-yāna, the path of the gods. The yogī, after death, does not travel along any path; having already attained the Highest, which has nothing to do with any particular place or time, he has no world to reach.

Supreme, etc.—The supreme Truth which the yogī attains after transcending all duality is ever present, eternal, and absolute, so cannot be spoken of in terms of relative existence or relative truth. When the sense of duality is destroyed, this Truth at once reveals itself, even as the sun is seen shining when clouds disperse.

तीर्थे वान्त्यजगेहे वा यत्र कुत्र मृतोऽपि वा ।
न योगी पश्यते गर्भं परे ब्रह्मणि लीयते ॥ २६ ॥

tīrthe vā antyaja-gehe vā yatra kutra mṛto'pi vā
na yogī paśyate garbhaṁ pare brahmaṇi līyate.

29. The yogī, having died anywhere, in a holy place or in the house of an untouchable, does not see the mother's womb again—he is dissolved in the supreme Brahman.

Does not, etc.—is not reborn.

सहजमजमचिन्त्यं यस्तु पश्येत्स्वरूपं
घटति यदि यथेष्टं लिप्यते नैव दोषैः।
सकृदपि तदभावात्कर्म किञ्चिन्नकुर्यात्
तदपि न च विबद्धः संयमी वा तपस्वी ॥ ३० ॥

sahajam ajam acintyaṁ yas tu paśyet svarūpaṁ
ghaṭati yadi yatheṣṭaṁ lipyate naiva doṣaiḥ
sakṛd api tadabhāvāt karma kiñcin na kuryāt
tad api na ca vibaddhaḥ samyamī vā tapasvī.

30. He who has seen his true Self, which is innate, unborn, and incomprehensible, does not, if anything desired happens to him, become tainted. Being free from taint, he never performs any action. The man of self-restraint or the ascetic, therefore, is never bound.

Desired, etc.—only apparently desired by him who possesses Self-knowledge. When one has attained to the knowledge of the Self one may still continue to live in the body and appear to be actively seeking desired objects. This, however, is only in semblance. Being free from the taint of ignorance, which makes the average man seek desirable objects and avoid undesirable ones, he is really inactive.

निरामयं निष्प्रतिमं निराकृति
निराश्रयं निर्वपुषं निराशिषम्।
निर्द्वन्द्वनिर्मोहमलुप्तशक्तिकं
तमीशमात्मानमुपैति शाश्वतम् ॥ ३१ ॥

nirāmayaṁ niṣpratimaṁ nirākṛtiṁ
nirāśrayaṁ nirvapuṣaṁ nirāśiṣam
nirdvandva-nirmoham alupta-śaktikaṁ
tam īśam ātmānam upaiti śāśvatam.

31. He attains to the supreme Self, who is eternal, pure, fearless, formless, and supportless, who is without body, without desire, beyond the pairs of opposites, free from illusion, and of undiminished power.

Pairs, etc.—such as heat and cold, pain and pleasure, ignorance and knowledge, life and death, which are all relative.

वेदो न दीक्षा न च मुण्डनक्रिया
गुरुर्न शिष्यो न च यन्त्रसम्पदः ।
मुद्रादिकं चापि न यत्र भासते
तमीशमात्मानमुपैति शाश्वतम् ॥ ३२ ॥

vedo na dīkṣā na ca muṇḍana-kriyā
gurur na śiṣyo na ca yantra saṁpadaḥ
mudrādikaṁ cāpi na yatra bhāsate
tam īśam ātmānam upaiti śāśvatam.

32. He attains to the supreme, eternal Self, in whom exists no Veda, no initiation, no tonsure, no teacher, no disciple, no perfection of

symbolic figures, no hand-posture or anything else.

Symbolic, etc.—In ritualistic worship geometrical figures drawn on metal, stone, etc., are sometimes used as symbols of Divinity.

Hand-posture—called mudra, used as part of ritualistic worship.

न शाम्भवं शाक्तिकमानवं न वा
पिण्डं च रूपं च पदादिकं न वा ।
आरम्भनिष्पत्तिघटादिकं च नो
तमीशमात्मानमुपैति शाश्वतम् ॥ ३३ ॥

na śāṁbhavaṁ śāktika-mānavaṁ na vā
piṇḍaṁ ca rūpaṁ ca padādikaṁ na vā
āraṁbha-niṣpatti ghaṭādikaṁ ca no
tam īśam aṭmānam upaiti śāśvatam.

33. He attains to the supreme, eternal Self, in whom is neither śāmbhavī, nor śāktī, nor ānavī initiation; neither a sphere, nor an image, nor a foot, nor anything else; neither beginning, nor ending, nor a jar, etc.

Śāmbhavī, etc.—Tāntrika texts speak of three kinds of initiation. Śāmbhavī initiation, which is very rare, is that in which the teacher by a mere word, look, touch, or by will imparts the highest knowledge of God to the disciple instantly. Śāktī initiation is that in which the teacher instills into the disciple a great spiritual power which will of itself, within a reasonable time, bring about the disciple's spiritual emancipation. The disciple does not have to exert himself for this realization. Such initiation also is exceptional. Ānavī or mantrī initiation is that in which the teacher, on an auspicious day, instructs the disciple concerning the method of spiritual practice he should follow, gives him a word or a phrase (called mantra) to repeat, and offers other necessary instructions. The disciple must practise according to these instructions to gain spiritual knowledge.

Sphere—a round symbol made of stone etc.

Foot—Sometimes either an image of a foot or a footprint is used as a symbol of worship.

Beginning,etc.—ceremonial beginning and ending of worship.

Jar—Sometimes a jar filled with water is used as a symbol of the all-pervading Divinity.

यस्य स्वरूपात्सचराचरं जगद्
उत्पद्यते तिष्ठति लीयतेऽपि वा ।
पयोविकारादिव फेनबुद्बुदा-
स्तमीशमात्मानमुपैति शाश्वतम् ॥ ३४ ॥

yasya svarūpāt sacarācaraṁ jagad
utpadyate tiṣṭhati līyate'pi vā
payo-vikārād iva phena-budbudās
tam īśam ātmānam upaiti śāśvatam.

34. He attains to the supreme, eternal Self, from whose essence the universe of movable and immovable objects is born, in whom it rests, and into whom it dissolves, even as foam and bubbles are born of the transformation of water.

नासानिरोधो न च दृष्टिरासनं
बोधोऽप्यबोधोऽपि न यत्र भासते ।
नाडीप्रचारोऽपि न यत्र किञ्चित्-
तमीशमात्मानमुपैति शाश्वतम् ॥ ३५ ॥

nāsā-nirodho na ca dṛṣṭir āsanaṁ
bodho'py abodho'pi na yatra bhāsate
nāḍī-pracāro'pi na yatra kiñcit
tam īśam ātmānam upaiti śāśvatam.

35. He attains to the supreme, eternal Self, in whom is no closing of nostril nor gazing nor posture, and in whom is neither knowledge nor ignorance nor any nerve-current.

Closing, etc.—In the practice of prāṇāyāma or breath control, each nostril in turn is closed with a finger in order to breathe only with the other nostril.

Gazing—fixing the eyes on a certain point to induce concentration.

Posture—a particular way of sitting which allows the body to be most comfortable and yet conduces to the practice of mental concentration.

Nerve-current—The reference is to the three nerves mentioned in Yoga texts—iḍā, piṅgalā, and suṣumnā—along which thought-currents are made to flow in order to realize higher states of consciousness.

नानात्वमेकत्वमुभत्वमन्यता
अणुत्वदीर्घत्वमहत्त्वशून्यता ।
मानत्वमेयत्वसमत्ववर्जितं
तमीशमात्मानमुपैति शाश्वतम् ॥ ३६ ॥

nānātvam ekatvam ubhatvam anyatā
aṇutva-dīrghatva-mahatva-śūnyatā
mānatva-meyatva-samatva-varjitaṁ
tam īśam ātmānam upaiti śāśvatam.

36. He attains to the supreme, eternal Self, who is devoid of manifoldness, oneness, many-and-oneness, and otherness; who is devoid of minuteness, length, largeness, and nothingness; who is devoid of knowledge, knowableness, and sameness.

सुसंयमी वा यदि वा न संयमी
सुसंग्रही वा यदि वा न संग्रही ।
निष्कर्मको वा यदि वा सकर्मक-
स्तमीशमात्मानमुपैति शाश्वतम् ॥ ३७ ॥

susaṁyamī vā yadi vā na saṁyamī
susaṅgrahī vā yadi vā na sangrahī
niṣkarmako vā yadi vā sakarmakaḥ
tam īśam ātmānam upaiti śāśvatam.

37. He attains the supreme, eternal Self whether he has perfect self-control or not, whether he has withdrawn his senses well or not, whether he has gone beyond activity or is active.

Has, etc.—whether he appears to have self-control or not.

मनो न बुद्धिर्न शरीरमिन्द्रियं
तन्मात्रभूतानि न भूतपञ्चकम् ।
अहंकृतिश्चापि वियत्स्वरूपकं
तमीशमात्मानमुपैति शाश्वतम् ॥ ३८ ॥

mano na buddhiḥ na śarīram indriyaṁ
tanmātra-bhūtāni na bhūta-pañcakam
ahaṁkṛtiś cāpi viyat-svarūpakaṁ
tam īśam ātmānam upaiti śāśvatam.

38. He attains the supreme, eternal Self who is not mind, intelligence, body, senses, or egoism; who is neither the subtle elements nor the five gross elements nor of the nature of space.

विधौ निरोधे परमात्मतां गते
न योगिनश्चेतसि भेदवर्जिते ।
शौचं न वाशौचमलिङ्गभावना
सर्वं विधेयं यदि वा निषिध्यते ।। ३९ ।।

vidhau nirodhe paramātmatāṁ gate
na yoginaś cetasi bhedavarjite
śaucaṁ na vāśaucam aliṅgabhāvanā
sarvaṁ vidheyaṁ yadi vā niṣidhyate.

39. When injunctions cease and the yogī attains to the supreme Self, his mind being void of differentiations, he has neither purity nor impurity; his contemplation is without distinguishing attributes; and even what is usually prohibited is permissible to him.

Injunctions—prescriptions given by the scriptures to a spiritual aspirant in regard to what he should practise. The yogī who has attained to the Highest is beyond the need of such prescriptions.

Contemplation,etc.—The consciousness of the yogī dwells on the attributeless Absolute.

Prohibited,etc.—The spiritual aspirant is prohibited from doing certain things, just as he is enjoined to do other things; but upon attaining the Highest he goes beyond all injunctions and prohibitions. Realizing himself as the Absolute, he may act in even an apparently evil way, just as God does some apparently evil things in His creation.

मनो वचो यत्र न शक्तमीरितुं
नूनं कथं तत्र गुरूपदेशता ।
इमां कथामुक्तवतो गुरोस्तद्-
युक्तस्य तत्त्वं हि समं प्रकाशते ॥ ४० ॥

mano vaco yatra na śaktam īrituṁ
nūnaṁ kathaṁ tatra gurūpadeśatā
imāṁ kathām uktavato guroḥ tad
yuktasya tattvaṁ hi samaṁ prakāśate.

40. Where mind and speech can utter nothing, how can there be instruction by a teacher? To the teacher—ever united with Brahman—who has said these words, the homogeneous Truth shines out.

CHAPTER III

गुणविगुणविभागो वर्तते नैव किञ्चित्
रतिविरतिविहीनं निर्मलं निष्प्रपञ्चम् ।
गुणविगुणविहीनं व्यापकं विश्वरूपं
कथमहमिह वन्दे व्योमरूपं शिवं वै ॥ १ ॥

guṇa-viguṇa-vibhāgo vartate naiva kiñcit
rati-virati-vihīnaṁ nirmalaṁ niṣprapañcam
guṇa-viguṇa-vihīnaṁ vyāpakaṁ viśva-rūpaṁ
katham aham iha vande vyoma-rūpaṁ śivaṁ vai

1. The distinction of quality and absence of quality does not exist in the least. How shall I worship Śiva (the Absolute) who is devoid of quality and absence of quality, who is devoid of attachment and detachment, who is of the form of ether, omniform, beyond illusion, and all-pervading?

Distinction, etc.—In this discourse the Avadhūta describes the Self as neither distinct from phenomenal existence nor identical with it. Such a perception of the Self is the highest realization conceivable, inasmuch as the consciousness of Oneness is so full that any recognition of even the least distinction is impossible. This Self is the same as Brahman. It is I. When the knowledge of this Self comes, even the so-called relative existence is no longer the same as it appears to the ignorant. "Quality" refers to the different attributes belonging to relative objects, which are due to the three basic qualities, sattva, rajas, and tamas. While relative existences have quality, the Absolute is beyond all quality. This distinction, however, is the language of relative consciousness. In the state of Self-realization to which we referred above, such distinction does not exist.

Worship—Worship implies duality, at least, distinction.

श्वेतादिवर्णरहितो नियतं शिवश्च
कार्यं हि कारणमिदं हि परं शिवश्च ।
एवं विकल्परहितोऽहमलं शिवश्च
स्वात्मानमात्मनि सुमित्र कथं नमामि ॥ २ ॥

śvetādi-varṇa-rahito niyataṁ śivaś ca
kāryaṁ hi kāraṇam idaṁ hi paraṁ śivaś ca
evaṁ vikalparahito'ham alaṁ śivaśca
svātmānam ātmani sumitra kathaṁ namāmi

2. Siva (the Absolute) is ever without white and other colours. This effect and cause are also the supreme Śiva. I am thus the pure Siva, devoid of all doubt. O beloved friend, how shall I bow to my own Self in my Self?

White, etc.—Although the term "Śiva" in the present text means the Absolute, it is also a name of the personal God with form. He is then supposed to have a white complexion.

Effect—the universe.

Doubt—that is to say, about the knowledge of Self and Truth.

निर्मूलमूलरहितो हि सदोदितोऽहं
निर्धूमधूमरहितो हि सदोदितोऽहम् ।
निर्दीपदीपरहितो हि सदोदितोऽहं
ज्ञानामृतं समरसं गगनोपमोऽहम् ॥ ३ ॥

nirmūla-mūla-rahito hi sadodito'haṁ
nirdhūma-dhūma-rahito hi sadodito'ham
nirdīpa-dīpa-rahito hi sadodito'haṁ
jñānāmṛtaṁ samarasaṁ gaganopamo'ham.

3. I am devoid of root and rootlessness and am ever manifest. I am devoid of smoke and smokelessness and am ever manifest. I am devoid of light and absence of light and am ever manifest. I am the nectar of Knowledge, homogeneous Existence, like the sky.

Devoid, etc.—"Root" means cause. The Avadhūta is describing the Self in Its absolute aspect as well as in Its aspect of manifestation.

Smoke—the envelope of māyā.

Light—relative knowledge.

निष्काममकाममिह नाम कथं वदामि
निःसङ्गसङ्गमिह नाम कथं वदामि ।
निःसारसाररहितं च कथं वदामि
ज्ञानामृतं समरसं गगनोपमोऽहम् ॥ ४ ॥

niṣkāma-kāmam iha nāma kathaṁ vadāmi
nissaṅga-saṅgam iha nāma kathaṁ vadāmi
nissāra-sara-rahitaṁ ca kathaṁ vadāmi
jñānāmṛtaṁ samarasaṁ gaganopamo'ham.

4. How shall I speak of desirelessness and desire? How shall I speak of nonattachment and attachment? How shall I speak of Him as devoid of substance and insubstantiality? I am the nectar of Knowledge, homogeneous Existence, like the sky.

How, etc.—No description or conception is possible of that Self-realization in which there is no distinction of quality or absence of quality.

Substance, etc.—transcendental Reality; "insubstantiality"—relative reality.

अद्वैतरूपमखिलं हि कथं वदामि
द्वैतस्वरूपमखिलं हि कथं वदामि ।
नित्यं त्वनित्यमखिलं हि कथं वदामि
ज्ञानामृतं समरसं गगनोपमोऽहम् ॥ ५ ॥

advaita-rūpam akhilaṁ hi kathaṁ vadāmi
dvaita-svarūpam akhilaṁ hi kathaṁ vadāmi
nityaṁ tvanityam akhilaṁ hi kathaṁ vadāmi
jñanāmṛtaṁ samarasaṁ gaganopamo'ham.

5. How shall I speak of the Whole, which is nondual? How shall I speak of the Whole, which is of the nature of duality? How shall I speak of the Whole, which is eternal and non-eternal? I am the nectar of Knowledge, homogeneous Existence, like the sky.

How, etc.—It is not possible to describe the Self even in Its phenomenal aspect, because thought or language can comprehend even phenomena only in their superficial aspects. In their deeper aspects phenomena are indistinguishable from the transcendental Self and therefore indescribable.

स्थूलं हि नो नहि कृशं न गतागतं हि
आद्यन्तमध्यरहितं न परापरं हि ।
सत्यं वदामि खलु वै परमार्थतत्त्वं
ज्ञानामृतं समरसं गगनोपमोऽहम् ॥ ६ ॥

sthūlaṁ hi no nahi kṛśaṁ na gatāgataṁ hi
ādyanta-madhya-rahitaṁ na parāparaṁ hi
satyaṁ vadāmi khalu vai paramārtha-tattvaṁ
jñānāmṛtaṁ samarasaṁ gaganopamo'ham.

6. It is neither gross nor subtle. It has neither come nor gone. It is without beginning, middle,

and end. It is neither high nor low. I am truly declaring the highest Truth and Reality—I am the nectar of Knowledge, homogeneous Existence, like the sky.

Come, etc.—The Self, even when It appears to manifest relative existence, does not really do so.

संविद्धि सर्वकरणानि नभोनिभानि
संविद्धि सर्वविषयांश्च नभोनिभांश्च ।
संविद्धि चैकममलं न हि बन्धमुक्तं
ज्ञानामृतं समरसं गगनोपमोऽहम् ॥ ७ ॥

saṁviddhi sarva-karaṇāni nabho-nibhāni
saṁviddhi sarva-viṣayāṁś ca nabho-nibhaś ca
saṁviddhi caikam amalaṁ na hi bandhamuktaṁ
jñānāmṛtaṁ samarasaṁ gaganopamo'ham.

7. Know all instruments of perception to be like ethereal space. Know all objects of perception to be like ethereal space. Know this pure One as neither bound nor free. I am the nectar of Knowledge, homogeneous Existence, like the sky.

Like, etc.—The instruments of perception—senses, mind, etc.—are not what they seem to us in ignorance. They also are formless Consciousness Itself.

दुर्बोधबोधगहनो न भवामि तात
दुर्लक्ष्यलक्ष्यगहनो न भवामि तात ।
आसन्नरूपगहनो न भवामि तात
ज्ञानामृतं समरसं गगनोपमोऽहम् ॥ ८ ॥

durbodha bodha-gahano na bhavāmi tāta
durlakṣya lakṣya-gahano na bhavāmi tāta
āsanna-rūpa-gahano na bhavāmi tāta
jñānamṛtaṁ samarasaṁ gaganopamo'ham.

8. My child, I am not difficult to comprehend, nor am I hidden in consciousness. My child, I am not difficult to perceive, nor am I hidden in the perceptible. My child, I am not hidden in the forms immediately near me. I am the nectar of Knowledge, homogeneous Existence, like the sky.

निष्कर्मकर्मदहनो ज्वलनो भवामि
निर्दुःखदुःखदहनो ज्वलनो भवामि ।
निर्देहदेहदहनो ज्वलनो भवामि
ज्ञानामृतं समरसं गगनोपमोऽहम् ॥ ९ ॥

niṣkarma-karma-dahano jvalano bhavāmi
nirduḥkha-duḥkha-dahano jvalano bhavāmi
nirdeha-deha-dahano jvalano bhavāmi
jñānāmṛtaṁ samarasaṁ gaganopamo'ham.

9. I am the fire that burns the karma of one who is beyond all karma. I am the fire that burns the sorrow of one beyond all sorrow. I am the fire that burns the body of one who is devoid of body. I am the nectar of Knowledge, homogeneous Existence, like the sky.

I,etc.—In verses 9 and 10, the Self is being described as the negation of any adjuncts that seem to limit It.

निष्पापपापदहनो हि हुताशनोऽहं
निर्धर्मधर्मदहनो हि हुताशनोऽहम् ।
निर्बन्धबन्धदहनो हि हुताशनोऽहं
ज्ञानामृतं समरसं गगनोपमोऽहम् ॥ १० ॥

niṣpāpa-pāpa-dahano hi hutāśano'haṁ
nirdharma-dharma-dahano hi hutāśano'ham
nirbandha-bandha-dahano hi hutāśano'haṁ
jñānāmṛtaṁ samarasaṁ gaganopamo'ham.

10. I am the fire that burns the sin of one who is sinless. I am the fire that burns the attributes of one who is without attributes. I am the fire that burns the bondage of one who is without bondage. I am the nectar of Knowledge, homogeneous Existence, like the sky.

निर्भवभावरहितो न भवामि वत्स
निर्योगयोगरहितो न भवामि वत्स ।

निश्चित्तचित्तरहितो न भवामि वत्स
ज्ञानामृतं समरसं गगनोपमोऽहम् ॥ ११ ॥

nirbhāva-bhāvarahito na bhavāmi vatsa
niryoga-yoga-rahito na bhavāmi vatsa
niścitta-citta-rahito na bhavāmi vatsa
jñānāmṛtaṁ samarasaṁ gaganopamo'ham.

11. My child, I am not devoid of nonexistence and existence. My child, I am not devoid of unity and absence of unity. My child, I am not devoid of mind and absence of mind. I am the nectar of Knowledge, homogeneous Existence, like the sky.

Nonexistence—"Existence" here is relative existence.

Unity—transcendental Oneness.

Unity—organic unity,as in the phenomenal universe.

Devoid,etc.—in the relative and the transcendental states of the Self, respectively.

निर्मोहमोहपदवीति न मे विकल्पो
निःशोकशोकपदवीति न मे विकल्पः ।
निर्लोभलोभपदवीति न मे विकल्पो
ज्ञानामृतं समरसं गगनोपमोऽहम् ॥ १२ ॥

nirmoha-moha-padavīti na me vikalpaḥ
niśśoka-śoka-padavīti na me vikalpaḥ
nirlobha-lobha-padavīti na me vikalpaḥ
jñānāmṛtaṁ samarasaṁ gaganopamo'ham.

12. It is not my ignorance that the One beyond illusion seems to be posited in illusion. It is not my ignorance that the griefless One appears to be posited in grief. It is not my ignorance that the greedless One appears to be posited in greed. I am the nectar of Knowledge, homogeneous Existence, like the sky.

Not, etc.—The truth is that the Self alone is transcendental and immutable; yet to the ignorant It appears to be involved in the relative existence. The Self, however, cannot be considered responsible for this appearance, because by Its very nature It is beyond illusion.

संसारसन्ततिलता न च मे कदाचित्
सन्तोषसन्ततिसुखो न च मे कदाचित् ।
अज्ञानबन्धनमिदं न च मे कदाचित्
ज्ञानामृतं समरसं गगनोपमोऽहम् ॥ १३ ॥

saṁsāra-santati-latā na ca me kadācit
saṁtoṣa-santati-sukho na ca me kadācit
ajñāna-bandhanam idaṁ na ca me kadācit
jñānāmṛtaṁ samarasaṁ gaganopamo'ham.

13. The creeperlike growth of worldly existence is never mine. The joy of extended contentment is never mine. This bondage of ignorance is never mine. I am the nectar of Knowledge, homogeneous Existence, like the sky.

Contentment—in worldly existence.

संसारसन्ततिरजो न च मे विकारः
सन्तापसन्ततितमो न च मे विकारः ।
सत्त्वं स्वधर्मजनकं न च मे विकारो
ज्ञानामृतं समरसं गगनोपमोऽहम् ॥ १४ ॥

saṁsāra-santati-rajo na ca me vikāraḥ
santāpa-santati-tamo na ca me vikāraḥ
sattvaṁ svadharma-janakaṁ na ca me vikāraḥ
jñānamṛtaṁ samarasaṁ gaganopamo'ham.

14. The activity involved in the extension of relative existence is not a modification of myself. The gloom which is the expansion of grief is not a modification of myself. The tranquillity which produces one's religious merit is not a modification of mine. I am the nectar of Knowledge, homogeneous Existence, like the sky.

Activity—the quality of rajas through which worldly existence continues.

Gloom—the quality of tamas which is considered to be the cause of sorrow.

Tranquillity—the quality of sattva.

सन्तापदुःखजनको न विधिः कदाचित्
सन्तापयोगजनितं न मनः कदाचित् ।

यस्मादहङ्कृतिरियं न च मे कदाचित्
ज्ञानामृतं समरसं गगनोपमोऽहम् ॥ १५ ॥

santāpa-duḥkha-janako na vidhiḥ kadācit
santāpa-yoga-janitaṁ na manaḥ kadācit
yasmād ahaṅkṛtiriyaṁ na ca me kadācit
jñānāmṛtaṁ samarasaṁ gaganopamo'ham.

15. I have never any action which is the cause of regret and misery. Mine is never a mind which is the product of the experience of misery. Since this egoism never is mine, I am the nectar of Knowledge, homogeneous Existence, like the sky.

निष्कम्पकम्पनिधनं न विकल्पकल्पं
स्वप्नप्रबोधनिधनं न हिताहितं हि ।
निःसारसारनिधनं न चराचरं हि
ज्ञानामृतं समरसं गगनोपमोऽहम् ॥ १६ ॥

niṣkaṁpa-kaṁpa-nidhanaṁ na vikalpa-kalpaṁ
svapna-prabodha-nidhanaṁ na hitāhitaṁ hi
nissāra-sāra-nidhanaṁ na carācaraṁ hi
jñānāmṛtaṁ samarasaṁ gaganopamo'ham

16. I am the death of the movement of the unmoving One. I am neither decision nor indecision. I am the death of sleep and wakeful-

ness. I am neither good nor evil, neither the moving nor the unmoving. I am the death of the substance of the insubstantial. I am the nectar of Knowledge, homogeneous Existence, like the sky.

Death—negation.

Movement—projection of the manifold universe.

Decision,etc.—Decision and indecision are both states of mind and, therefore, not the transcendental Self.

Insubstantial—māyā, which is unreal.

नो वेद्यवेदकमिदं न च हेतुतर्क्यं
वाचामगोचरमिदं न मनो न बुद्धिः ।
एवं कथं हि भवतः कथयामि तत्त्वं
ज्ञानामृतं समरसं गगनोपमोऽहम् ॥ १७ ॥

no vedya-vedakam idaṁ na ca hetu-tarkyaṁ
vacāmagocaram idaṁ na mano na buddhiḥ
evaṁ kathaṁ hi bhavataḥ kathayāmi tattvaṁ
jñānāmṛtaṁ samarasaṁ gaganopamo'ham.

17. This (Self) is neither knowable nor the instrument of knowing. It is neither reason nor the one to be reasoned about. It is beyond the reach of words. It is neither mind nor intelligence. How then can I speak this Truth to you? I am the nectar of Knowledge, homogeneous Existence, like the sky.

निर्भिन्नभिन्नरहितं परमार्थतत्त्व-
मन्तर्बहिर्न हि कथं परमार्थतत्त्वम् ।
प्राक्सम्भवं न च रतं नहि वस्तु किञ्चित्
ज्ञानामृतं समरसं गगनोपमोऽहम् ॥ १८ ॥

nirbhinna-bhinna-rahitaṁ paramārtha-tattvaṁ
antar bahir na hi kathaṁ paramārtha-tattvam
prāk saṁbhavaṁ na ca rataṁ na hi vastu kiñcit
jñānāmṛtaṁ samarasaṁ gaganopamo'ham.

18. The supreme Reality is devoid of the undivided and the divided. The supreme Truth is in no way within or without. It is beyond causation. It is not attached, nor is It any substance. I am the nectar of Knowledge, homogeneous Existence, like the sky.

Undivided, etc.—unity and variety. Even unity is within the realm of relativity since it implies, by contrast, variety.

Attached—related to, or associated with, name and form.

रागादिदोषरहितं त्वहमेव तत्त्वं
दैवादिदोषरहितं त्वहमेव तत्त्वं ।
संसारशोकरहितं त्वहमेव तत्त्वं
ज्ञानामृतं समरसं गगनोपमोऽहम् ॥ १९ ॥

ragādi-doṣa-rahitaṁ tvaham eva tattvaṁ
daivādi-doṣa-rahitaṁ tvaham eva tattvam

samsāra-śoka-rahitaṁ tvaham eva tattvaṁ
jñānāmṛtaṁ samarasaṁ gaganopamo'ham.

19. I am verily the Reality, free of such blemishes as attachment. I am verily the Reality, free of such blemishes as destiny. I am verily the Reality, free of the grief caused by transmigratory existence. I am the nectar of Knowledge, homogeneous Existence, like the sky.

Destiny—It implies time, process, and compulsion; therefore it cannot be true of the Self.

स्थानत्रयं यदि च नेति कथं तुरीयं
कालत्रयं यदि च नेति कथं दिशश्च ।
शान्तं पदं हि परमं परमार्थतत्त्वं
ज्ञानामृतं समरसं गगनोपमोऽहम् ॥ २० ॥

sthāna-trayaṁ yadi ca neti kathaṁ turīyaṁ
kāla-trayaṁ yadi ca neti kathaṁ diśaś ca
śāntaṁ padaṁ hi paramaṁ paramārtha-tattvaṁ
jñānāmṛtaṁ samarasaṁ gaganopamo'ham.

20. If there are no three planes (of existence), how can there be the fourth? If there are no three times, how can there be quarters? The supreme Reality is the state of the highest serenity. I am the nectar of Knowledge, homogeneous Existence, like the sky.

Fourth—The transcendental state is called "turīya," or the fourth, in relation to the three other states—the waking, dream, and deep-sleep; but such a designation implies relativity and is therefore not true of the Self.

Three,etc.—past, present, and future.

Quarters—space.

दीर्घो लघुः पुनरितीह नमे विभागो
विस्तारसंकटमितीह न मे विभागः ।
कोणं हि वर्तुलमितीह न मे विभागो
ज्ञानामृतं समरसं गगनोपमोऽहम् ॥ २१ ॥

dīrgho laghuḥ punar itīha na me vibhāgo
vistāra saṅkaṭam itīha na me vibhāgaḥ
koṇaṁ hi vartulam itīha na me vibhāgaḥ
jñānāmṛtaṁ samarasaṁ gaganopamo'ham.

21. I have no such divisions as long or short. I have no such divisions as wide or narrow. I have no such divisions as angular or circular. I am the nectar of Knowledge, homogeneous Existence, like the sky.

मातापितादि तनयादि न मे कदाचित्
जातं मृतं न च मनो न च मे कदाचित् ।
निर्व्याकुलं स्थिरमिदं परमार्थतत्त्वं
ज्ञानामृतं समरसं गगनोपमोऽहम् ॥ २२ ॥

mātā pitādi tanayādi na me kadācit
jātaṁ mṛtaṁ na ca mano na ca me kadācit
nirvyākulaṁ sthiram idaṁ paramārtha-tattvaṁ
jñānāmṛtaṁ samarasaṁ gaganopamo'ham.

22. I never had a mother, father, son, or the like. I was never born and never did I die. I never had a mind. The supreme Reality is undistracted and calm. I am the nectar of Knowledge, homogeneous Existence, like the sky.

शुद्धं विशुद्धमविचारमनन्तरूपं
निर्लेपलेप-मविचारमनन्तरूपम् ।
निष्खण्डखण्डमविचारमनन्तरूपं
ज्ञानामृतं समरसं गगनोपमोऽहम् ॥ २३ ॥

śuddhaṁ viśuddham avicāram ananta-rūpaṁ
nirlepa-lepam avicāram ananta-rūpam
niṣkhaṇḍa-khaṇḍam avicāram ananta-rūpaṁ
jñānāmṛtaṁ samarasaṁ gaganopamo'ham.

23. I am pure, very pure—beyond reason and of infinite form. I am nonattachment and attachment—beyond reason and of infinite form. I am undivided and divided—beyond reason and of infinite form. I am the nectar of Knowledge, homogeneous Existence, like the sky.

ब्रह्मादयः सुरगणाः कथमत्र सन्ति
स्वर्गादयो वसतयः कथमत्र सन्ति ।
यद्येकरूपममलं परमार्थतत्त्वं
ज्ञानामृतं समरसं गगनोपमोऽहम् ॥ २४ ॥

brahmādayaḥ sura-gaṇāḥ katham atra santi
svargādayo vasatayaḥ katham atra santi
yady-ekarūpam amalaṁ paramārtha-tattvaṁ
jñānāmṛtaṁ samarasaṁ gaganopamo'ham.

24. If the supreme Reality is only one and stainless, how can there be here the hosts of gods beginning with Brahmā, and how can there be here the worlds of habitation, such as heaven? I am the nectar of Knowledge, homogeneous Existence, like the sky.

निर्नेति नेति विमलो हि कथं वदामि
निःशेषशेषविमलो हि कथं वदामि ।
निर्लिङ्गलिङ्गविमलो हि कथं वदामि
ज्ञानामृतं समरसं गगनोपमोऽहम् ॥ २५ ॥

nirneti neti vimalo hi kathaṁ vadāmi
niśśeṣa śeṣa vimalo hi kathaṁ vadāmi
nirliṅga liṅga vimalo hi kathaṁ vadāmi
jñānāmṛtaṁ samarasaṁ gaganopamo'ham.

25. How shall I, the pure One, the "not this" and yet the not "not this" speak? How shall I,

the pure One, the endless and the end, speak? How shall I, the pure One, attributeless and attribute, speak? I am the nectar of Knowledge, homogeneous Existence, like the sky.

"*Not this*"; *etc.*—The Self is spoken of in the Sruti as "neti, neti", "not this," "not this", for nothing can be predicated of the Self. Although such a negative determination of the Self is the best possible for thought, it still is tinged with relativity. In order to eliminate it, the Self is being spoken of as "the not 'not this'." Such a dual description also may mean that the Self is both "not this" as well as "this," i.e. the world of manifestation.

End—the negation of relativity.

Attribute—The Self not only appears as endowed with attribute, but it is also attribute itself.

निष्कर्मकर्मपरमं सततं करोमि
निःसङ्गसङ्गरहितं परमं विनोदम् ।
निर्देहदेहरहितं सततं विनोदं
ज्ञानामृतं समरसं गगनोपमोऽहम् ॥ २६ ॥

niṣkarma-karma-paramaṁ satataṁ karomi
nissaṅga-saṅga-rahitaṁ paramaṁ vinodaṁ
nirdeha-deha-rahitaṁ satataṁ vinodaṁ
jñānāmṛtaṁ samarasaṁ gaganopamo'ham.

26. I ever perform the supreme action which is nonaction. I am the supreme Joy, devoid of

attachment and detachment. I am the everlasting Joy, devoid of body and absence of body. I am the nectar of Knowledge, homogeneous Existence, like the sky.

Devoid,etc.—"Devoid of body" implies consciousness of body. In order to negate even this consciousness, the Self is being spoken of as being devoid of absence of body.

मायाप्रपञ्चरचना न च मे विकारः
कौटिल्यदम्भरचना न च मे विकारः।
सत्यानृतेति रचना न च मे विकारो
ज्ञानामृतं समरसं गगनोपमोऽहम् ॥ २७ ॥

māyā-prapañca-racanā na ca me vikāraḥ
kauṭilya-dambha-racanā na ca me vikāraḥ
satyānṛteti-racanā na ca me vikāro
jñānāmṛtaṁ samarasaṁ gaganopamo'ham.

27. The creation of the illusory universe is not my modification. The creation of deceit and arrogance is not my modification. The creation of truth and falsehood is not my modification. I am the nectar of Knowledge, homogeneous Existence, like the sky.

सन्ध्यादिकालरहितं न च मे वियोगो-
ह्यन्तः प्रबोधरहितं बधिरो न मूकः।
एवं विकल्परहितं न च भावशुद्धं
ज्ञानामृतं समरसं गगनोपमोऽहम् ॥ २८ ॥

sandhyādi-kāla-rahitaṁ na ca me viyogo
hyantaḥ-prabodha-rahitaṁ badhiro na mūkaḥ
evaṁ vikalpa-rahitaṁ na ca bhāva-śuddhaṁ
jñānāmṛtaṁ samarasaṁ gaganopamo'ham.

28. I am devoid of time, such as twilight—I have no disjunction. I am devoid of interiorness and awakening. I am neither deaf nor mute. I am thus devoid of illusion. I am not made pure by moods of mind. I am the nectar of Knowledge, homogeneous Existence, like the sky.

Am,etc.—The purity spoken of the Self is not a state of mind attained through effort; it is the very essence of the Self.

निर्नाथनाथरहितं हि निराकुलं वै
निश्चित्तचित्तविगतं हि निराकुलं वै ।
संविद्धि सर्वविगतं हि निराकुलं वै
ज्ञानामृतं समरसं गगनोपमोऽहम् ॥ २९ ॥

nirnātha-nātha-rahitaṁ hi nirākulaṁ vai
niścitta-citta-vigataṁ hi nirākulaṁ vai
saṁviddhi sarva-vigataṁ hi nirākulaṁ vai
jñānāmṛtaṁ samarasaṁ gaganopamo'ham.

29. I am without a master and the absence of a master—I am unperturbed. I have transcended mind and absence of mind—I am unperturbed.

Know me as unperturbed and transcendent of all. I am the nectar of Knowledge, homogeneous Existence, like the sky.

Without, etc.—The Self is absolutely independent, there being nothing other than the Self. The "absence of a master" is spoken of for the reason stated in the notes to verses 25 and 26.

Unperturbed—unaffected.

कान्तारमन्दिरमिदं हि कथं वदामि
संसिद्धसंशयमिदं हि कथं वदामि ।
एवं निरन्तरसमं हि निराकुलं वै
ज्ञानामृतं समरस गगनोपमोऽहम् ॥ ३० ॥

kāntāra-mandiram idaṁ hi kathaṁ vadāmi
saṁsiddha-saṁśayam idaṁ hi kathaṁ vadāmi
evaṁ nirantara-samaṁ hi nirākulaṁ vai
jñānāmṛtaṁ samarasaṁ gaganopamo'ham.

30. How shall I say that this is a forest or a temple? How shall I say that this is proved or doubtful? It is thus one uninterrupted, homogeneous, calm Existence. I am the nectar of Knowledge, homogeneous Existence, like the sky.

This—the immediate object of perception. For one who knows himself as the Self, all existence is the Self.

निर्जीवजीवरहितं सततं विभाति
निर्बीजबीजरहितं सततं विभाति ।
निर्वाणबन्धरहितं सततं विभाति
ज्ञानामृतं समरसं गगनोपमोऽहम् ॥ ३१ ॥

nirjīva-jīva-rahitaṁ satataṁ vibhāti
nirbīja-bīja-rahitaṁ satataṁ vibhāti
nirvāṇa-bandha-rahitaṁ satataṁ vibhāti
jñānāmṛtaṁ samarasaṁ gaganopamo'ham

31. (The Self), devoid of life and lifelessness, shines forever. Devoid of seed and seedlessness, of liberation and bondage, It shines forever. I am the nectar of Knowledge, homogeneous Existence, like the sky.

Life, etc.—Life and lifelessness are in the realm of the relative and therefore do not exist in the Self.

Seed, etc.—By "seed" is meant cause or origin of relative existence. "Seedlessness" is also relative by implication, being the opposite of seed.

सम्भूतिवर्जितमिदं सततं विभाति
संसारवर्जितमिदं सततं विभाति ।
संहारवर्जितमिदं सततं विभाति
ज्ञानामृत समरस गगनोपमोऽहम् ॥ ३२ ॥

saṁbhūti-varjitam idaṁ satataṁ vibhāti
saṁsāra-varjitam idaṁ satataṁ vibhāti

saṁhāra-varjitam idaṁ satataṁ vibhāti
jñānāmṛtaṁ samarasaṁ gaganopamo'ham.

32. It shines forever, devoid of birth, mundane existence, and death. I am the nectar of Knowledge, homogeneous Existence, like the sky.

उल्लेखमात्रमपि ते न च नामरूपं
निर्भिन्नभिन्नमपि ते न हि वस्तु किञ्चित् ।
निर्लज्जमानस करोषि कथं विषादं
ज्ञानामृतं समरसं गगनोपमोऽहम् ॥ ३३ ॥

ullekhamātram api te na ca nāma-rūpaṁ
nirbhinna-bhinnam api te na hi vastu kiñcit
nirlajja-mānasa karoṣi kathaṁ viṣādaṁ
jñānāmṛtaṁ samarasaṁ gaganopamo'ham.

33. Thou hast no name and form even to the extent of allusion, nor any substance differentiated or undifferentiated. Why dost thou grieve, O thou of shameless mind? I am the nectar of Knowledge, homogeneous Existence, like the sky.

Substance, etc.—relative reality, manifest or unmanifest.

किं नाम रोदिषि सखे न जरा न मृत्युः
किं नाम रोदिषि सखे न च जन्मदुःखम् ।

किं नाम रोदिषि सखे न च ते विकारो
ज्ञानामृतं समरसं गगनोपमोऽहम् ॥ ३४ ॥

kiṁ nāma rodiṣi sakhe na jarā na mṛtyuḥ
kiṁ nāma rodiṣi sakhe na ca janma-duḥkham
kiṁ nāma rodiṣi sakhe na ca te vikāraḥ
jñānāmṛtaṁ samarasaṁ gaganopamo'ham.

34. Why weepest thou, friend? Thou hast no old age or death. Why weepest thou, friend? Thou hast no misery of birth. Why weepest thou, friend? There is no change for thee. I am the nectar of Knowledge, homogeneous Existence, like the sky.

किं नाम रोदिषि सखे न च ते स्वरूपं
किं नाम रोदिषि सखे न च ते विरूपम् ।
किं नाम रोदिषि सखे न च ते वयांसि
ज्ञानामृतं समरसं गगनोपमोऽहम्. ॥ ३५ ॥

kiṁ nāma rodiṣi sakhe na ca te svarūpaṁ
kiṁ nāma rodiṣi sakhe na ca te virūpam
kiṁ nāma rodiṣi sakhe na ca te vayāṁsi
jñānāmṛtaṁ samarasaṁ gaganopamo'ham.

35. Why dost thou weep, friend? Thou hast no natural form. Why dost thou weep, friend? Thou hast no deformity. Why dost thou weep, friend? Thou hast no age. I am the nectar of

Knowledge, homogeneous Existence, like the sky.

किं नाम रोदिषि सखे न च ते वयांसि
किं नाम रोदिषि सखे न च ते मनांसि ।
किं नाम रोदिषि सखे न तवेन्द्रियाणि
ज्ञानामृतं समरसं गगनोपमोऽहम् ॥ ३६ ॥

kiṁ nāma rodiṣi sakhe na ca te vayāṁsi
kiṁ nāma rodiṣi sakhe na ca te manāṁsi
kiṁ nāma rodiṣi sakhe na tavendriyāṇi
jñānāmṛtaṁ samarasaṁ gaganopamo'ham.

36. Why dost thou weep, friend? Thou hast no age. Why dost thou weep, friend? Thou hast no mind. Why dost thou weep, friend? Thou hast no senses. I am the nectar of Knowledge, homogeneous Existence, like the sky.

किं नाम रोदिषि सखे न च तेऽस्ति कामः
किं नाम रोदिषि सखे न च ते प्रलोभः ।
किं नाम रोदिषि सखे न च ते विमोहो
ज्ञानामृतं समरसं गगनोपमोऽहम् ॥ ३७ ॥

kiṁ nāma rodiṣi sakhe na ca te'sti kāmaḥ
kiṁ nāma rodiṣi sakhe na ca te pralobhaḥ
kiṁ nāma rodiṣi sakhe na ca te vimohaḥ
jñānāmṛtaṁ samarasaṁ gaganopamo'ham.

37. Why dost thou weep, friend? Thou hast no lust. Why dost thou weep, friend? Thou hast no greed. Why dost thou weep, friend? Thou hast no delusion. I am the nectar of Knowledge, homogeneous Existence, like the sky.

ऐश्वर्यमिच्छसि कथं न च ते धनानि
ऐश्वर्यमिच्छसि कथं न च ते हि पत्नी ।
ऐश्वर्यमिच्छसि कथं न च ते ममेति
ज्ञानामृतं समरसं गगनोपमोऽहम् ॥ ३८ ॥

aiśvaryam icchasi kathaṁ na ca te dhanāni
aiśvaryam icchasi kathaṁ na ca te hi patnī
aiśvaryam icchasi kathaṁ na ca te mameti
jñānāmṛtaṁ samarasaṁ gaganopamo'ham.

38. Why dost thou desire affluence? Thou hast no wealth. Why dost thou desire affluence? Thou hast no wife. Why dost thou desire affluence? Thou hast none who is thine own. I am the nectar of Knowledge, homogeneous Existence, like the sky.

लिङ्गप्रपञ्चजनुषी न च ते न मे च
निर्लज्जमानसमिदं च विभाति भिन्नम् ।
निर्भेदभेदरहितं न च ते न मे च
ज्ञानामृतं समरसं गगनोपमोऽहम् ॥ ३९ ॥

liṅga-prapañca-januṣī na ca te na me ca
nirlajja-mānasam idaṁ ca vibhāti bhinnam
nirbheda-bheda-rahitaṁ na ca te na me ca
jñānāmṛtaṁ samarasaṁ gaganopamo'ham.

39. Birth in this universe of false appearances is neither thine nor mine. This shameless mind appears as differentiated. This, devoid of difference and nondifference, is neither mine nor thine. I am the nectar of Knowledge, homogeneous Existence, like the sky.

This—the Self.
Mine,etc.—The Self is not personal.

नो वाणुमात्रमपि ते हि विरागरूपं
नो वाणमात्रमपि ते हि सरागरूपम् ।
नो वाणुमात्रमपि ते हि सकामरूपं
ज्ञानामृतं समरसं गगनोपमोऽहम् ॥ ४ ॥

novāṇumātram api te hi virāga-rūpaṁ
novāṇumātram api te hi sarāga-rūpam
novāṇumātram api te hi sakāma-rūpam
jñānāmṛtaṁ samarasaṁ gaganopamo'ham.

40. Thou hast not the nature of nonattachment in the slightest, nor hast thou in the slightest the nature of attachment. Thou hast not even the slightest of the nature of desire. I am the nectar of Knowledge, homogeneous Existence, like the sky.

ध्याता न ते हि हृदये न च ते समाधि-
ध्यानं न ते हि हृदये न बाहिः प्रदेशः ।
ध्येयं न चेति हृदये न हि वस्तु कालो
ज्ञानामृतं समरसं गगनोपमोऽहम् ॥ ४१ ॥

dhyātā na te hi hṛdaye na ca te samādhir-
dhyānaṁ na te hi hṛdaye na bahiḥ pradeśaḥ
dhyeyaṁ na ceti hṛdaye na hi vastu kālo
jñānāmṛtaṁ samarasaṁ gaganopamo'ham.

41. In thy mind there is neither the meditator, meditation, nor the object of meditation. Thou hast no samādhi. There is no region outside thee, nor is there any substance or time. I am the nectar of Knowledge, homogeneous Existence, like the sky.

Meditator, etc.—All these imply relativity and therefore do not exist in absolute Consciousness.

यत्सारभूतमखिलं कथितं मया ते
न त्वं न मे न महतो न गुरुर्न शिष्यः ।
स्वच्छन्दरूपसहजं परमार्थतत्त्वं
ज्ञानामृतं समरसं गगनोपमोऽहम् ॥ ४२ ॥

yat sārabhūtam akhilaṁ kathitaṁ mayā te
na tvaṁ na me na mahato na gurur na śiṣyaḥ
svacchanda-rūpa-sahajaṁ paramārtha-tattvaṁ
jñānāmṛtaṁ samarasaṁ gaganopamo'ham.

42. I have told thee all that is essential. There is neither thou, nor anything for me or for a great one; nor is there any teacher or disciple. The supreme Reality is natural and exists in Its own way. I am the nectar of Knowledge, homogeneous Existence, like the sky.

Great, etc.—Not even he who has apprehension of supersensuous reality finds anything everlasting except the Self.

Natural—It is what It is.

कथमिह परमार्थं तत्त्वमानन्दरूपं
कथमिह परमार्थं नैवमानन्दरूपम् ।
कथमिह परमार्थं ज्ञानविज्ञानरूपं
यदि परमहमेकं वर्तते व्योमरूपम् ॥ ४३ ॥

katham iha paramārthaṁ tattvam ānanda-rūpaṁ
katham iha paramārthaṁ naivam ānanda-rūpam
katham iha paramārthaṁ jñāna-vijñāna-rūpaṁ
yadi param aham ekaṁ vartate vyoma-rūpam.

43. If I, the Supreme, of the nature of sky, alone exist, how can there be here the supreme Truth which is blissful Reality, how can there be here the supreme Truth which is not of the nature of bliss, and how can there be here the supreme Truth of the nature of knowledge and intuition?

How, etc.—When God is spoken of as existing in the world, He is described as an object, perceived by a subject who is different or at least distinct from God. Such a description of the divine Self, however, is erroneous.

दहनपवनहीनं विद्धि विज्ञानमेक-
मवनिजलविहीनं विद्धि विज्ञानरूपम् ।
समगमनविहीनं विद्धि विज्ञानमेकं
गगनमिव विशालं विद्धि विज्ञानमेकम् ॥ ४४ ॥

dahana-pavana-hīnaṁ viddhi vijñānam ekaṁ
avani-jala-vihīnaṁ viddhi vijñāna-rūpam
sama-gamana-vihīnaṁ viddhi vijñānam ekaṁ
gaganam iva viśālaṁ viddhi vijñānam ekam.

44. Know the One who is Consciousness and devoid of fire and air. Know the One of the nature of Consciousness, who is devoid of earth and water. Know the One of the nature of Consciousness, who is devoid of coming and going.

Fire, etc.—Earth, water, fire, air, and ether are constituents of relative existence. (*See Chapter One, verses 3 and 25.*)

Coming, etc.—birth and death.

न शून्यरूपं न विशून्यरूपं
न शुद्धरूपं न विशुद्धरूपम् ।

रूपं विरूपं न भवामि किञ्चित्
स्वरूपरूपं परमार्थतत्त्वम् ॥ ४५ ॥

na śūnya-rūpaṁ na viśūnya-rūpaṁ
na śuddha-rūpaṁ na viśuddha-rūpam
rūpaṁ virūpaṁ na bhavāmi kiñcit
svarūpa-rūpaṁ paramārtha tattvam.

45. I am neither of the nature of the void nor of the nature of the nonvoid. I am neither of pure nature nor of impure nature. I am neither form nor formlessness. I am the supreme Reality of the form of Its own nature.

मुञ्च मुञ्च हि संसारं त्यागं मुञ्च हि सर्वथा ।
त्यागात्यागविषं शुद्धममृतं सहजं ध्रुवम् ॥ ४६ ॥

muñca muñca hi saṁsāraṁ tyāgaṁ muñca hi sarvathā
tyāgātyāga-viṣaṁ śuddham amṛtaṁ sahajaṁ dhruvam.

46. Renounce the world in every way. Renounce renunciation in every way. Renounce the poison of renunciation and nonrenunciation. The Self is pure, immortal, natural, and immutable.

Renounce, etc.—The act of renunciation also belongs to relative life and therefore to ignorance.

Chapter IV

नावाहनं नैव विसर्जनं वा
पुष्पाणि पत्राणि कथं भवन्ति ।
ध्यानानि मन्त्राणि कथं भवन्ति
समासमं चैव शिवार्चनं च ॥ १ ॥

nāvāhanaṁ naiva visarjanaṁ vā
puṣpāṇi patrāṇi kathaṁ bhavanti
dhyānāni mantrāṇi kathaṁ bhavanti
samāsamaṁ caiva śivārcanaṁ ca.

1. There is neither invitation nor casting off; how can there be flowers, leaves, meditations, and recitation of sacred texts, and how can there be worship of Śiva, which is identity and difference?

Invitation,etc.—In the beginning of ceremonial worship, one invites the Deity with recitation of certain mantras or sacred texts. At the end of the worship, certain other texts are recited, which indicate the return of the Deity to his divine realm; if any image has been used in the worship, it is then cast into water.

Flowers,etc.—These are parts of offering and worship.

Identity,etc.—In the first part of worship the worshipper thinks of himself as identical with the Deity;

later on, however, he considers himself different from Him and goes through the details of external worship.

न केवलं बन्धविबन्धमुक्तो
न केवलं शुद्धविशुद्धमुक्तः ।
न केवलं योगवियोगमुक्तः
स वै विमुक्तो गगनोपमोऽहम् ॥ २ ॥

na kevalaṁ bandha-vibandha-mukto
na kevalaṁ śuddha-viśuddha-muktaḥ
na kevalaṁ yoga-viyoga-muktaḥ
sa vai vimukto gaganopamo'ham.

2. The Absolute is not liberated from bondage and obstruction. The Absolute is not purified, cleansed, and released. The Absolute is not liberated by union or separation. I am, indeed, the free One, like the sky.

Liberated—implying that the Self was actually in bondage, which is not true.

Union, etc.—The highest state of spiritual experience, in which one realizes oneself as the Absolute, is sometimes loosely described as the union of the individual and the universal Self or as the separation of the soul from prakṛti or nature. Such statements are illogical.

सञ्जायते सर्वमिदं हि तथ्यं
सञ्जायते सर्वमिदं वितथ्यम् ।
एवं विकल्पो मम नैव जातः
स्वरूपनिर्वाणमनामयोऽहम् ॥ ३ ॥

sañjāyate sarvam idaṁ hi tathyaṁ
sañjāyate sarvam idaṁ vitathyam
evaṁ vikalpo mama naiva jātaḥ
svarūpa-nirvāṇam anāmayo'ham.

3. I have developed no false notion that all this reality comes into existence or that all this unreality comes into existence. I am free from disease—my form has been extinguished.

All,etc.—that which we perceive.

My, etc.—In the absolute realization, no form, physical or mental, remains.

न साञ्जनं चैव निरञ्जनं वा
न चान्तरं वापि निरन्तरं वा ।
अन्तर्विभिन्नं न हि मे विभाति
स्वरूपनिर्वाणमनामयोऽहम् ॥ ४ ॥

na sāñjanaṁ caiva nirañjanaṁ vā
na cāntaraṁ vāpi nirantaraṁ vā
antarvibhinnaṁ na hi me vibhāti
svarūpa-nirvāṇam anāmayo'ham.

4. Stained, stainless, divided, undivided, differentiated—none of these appear to me. I am free from disease—my form has been extinguished.

अबोधबोधो मम नैव जातो
बोधस्वरूपं मम नैव जातम् ।
निर्बोधबोधं च कथं वदामि
स्वरूपनिर्वाणमनामयोऽहम् ॥ ५ ॥

abodha-bodho mama naiva jāto
bodha-svarūpaṁ mama naiva jātam
nirbodha-bodhaṁ ca kathaṁ vadāmi
svarūpa-nirvāṇam anāmayo'ham.

5. It has not happened that I, the ignorant one, have attained to Knowledge, nor has it happened that I have become of the nature of Knowledge. And how can I say that I have both ignorance and knowledge? I am free from disease—my form has been extinguished.

न धर्मयुक्तो न च पापयुक्तो
न बन्धयुक्तो न च मोक्षयुक्तः ।
युक्तं त्वयुक्तं न च मे विभाति
स्वरूपनिर्वाणमनामयोऽहम् ॥ ६ ॥

na dharma-yukto na ca pāpa-yukto
na bandha-yukto na ca mokṣa-yuktaḥ
yuktaṁ tu ayuktaṁ na ca me vibhāti
svarūpa-nirvāṇam anāmayo'ham.

6. It (the Self) does not appear to me as virtuous or sinful, as bound or liberated, nor does It appear to me as united or separated. I am free from disease—my form has been extinguished.

परापरं वा न च मे कदाचित्
मध्यस्थभावो हि न चारिमित्रम् ।
हिताहितं चापि कथं वदामि
स्वरूपनिर्वाणमनामयोऽहम् ॥ ७ ॥

parāparaṁ vā na ca me kadācit
madhyastha-bhāvo hi na cāri-mitram
hitāhitaṁ cāpi kathaṁ vadāmi
svarūpa-nirvāṇam anāmayo'ham.

7. I never have the high, low, or middle state. I have no friend or foe. How shall I speak of good and evil? I am free from disease—my form has been extinguished.

नोपासको नैवमुपास्यरूपं
न चोपदेशो न च मे क्रिया च ।
संवित्स्वरूपं च कथं वदामि
स्वरूपनिर्वाणमनामयोऽहम् ॥ ८ ॥

nopāsako naivam upāsya-rūpaṁ
na copadeśo na ca me kriyā ca
samvit-svarūpaṁ ca kathaṁ vadāmi
svarūpa-nirvāṇam anāmayo'ham.

8. I am not the worshipper or of the form of the worshipped. I have neither instruction nor practice. How shall I speak of myself who am of the nature of Consciousness? I am free from disease—my form has been extinguished.

Practice—spiritual exercise.

नो व्यापकं व्याप्यमिहास्ति किञ्चित्
न चालयं वापि निरालयं वा ।
अशून्यशून्यं च कथं वदामि
स्वरूपनिर्वाणमनामयोऽहम् ॥ ९ ॥

no vyāpakaṁ vyāpyam ihāsti kiñcit
na cālayaṁ vāpi nirālayaṁ vā
aśūnya-śūnyaṁ ca kathaṁ vadāmi
svarūpa-nirvāṇam anāmayo'ham.

9. There is nothing here which pervades or is pervaded. There is no abode nor is there the abodeless. How shall I speak of void and non-void? I am free from disease—my form has been extinguished.

Void—The Transcendental has been spoken of as the Void by the Buddhists.

न ग्राहको ग्राह्यकमेव किञ्चित्
न कारणं वा मम नैव कार्यम् ।
अचिन्त्यचिन्त्यं च कथं वदामि
स्वरूपनिर्वाणमनामयोऽहम् ॥ १० ॥

na grāhako grāhyakam eva kiñcit
na kāraṇaṁ vā mama naiva kāryam
acintya-cintyaṁ ca kathaṁ vadami
svarūpa-nirvāṇam anāmayo'ham.

10. There is no one to understand and nothing, indeed, to be understood. I have no cause and no effect. How shall I say that I am conceivable or inconceivable? I am free from disease—my form has been extinguished.

न भेदकं वापि न चैव भेद्यं
न वेदकं वा मम नैव वेद्यम् ।
गतागतं तात कथं वदामि
स्वरूपनिर्वाणमनामयोऽहम् ॥ ११ ॥

na bhedakaṁ vāpi na caiva bhedyaṁ
na vedakaṁ vā mama naiva vedyam
gatāgataṁ tāta kathaṁ vadāmi
svarūpa-nirvāṇam anāmayo'ham.

11. There is nothing dividing, nothing to be divided. I have nothing to know with and nothing to be known. How shall I then speak of coming and going, my child? I am free from disease—my form has been extinguished.

Coming, etc.—birth and death.

न चास्ति देहो न च मे विदेहो
बुद्धिर्मनो मे न हि चेन्द्रियाणि ।
रागो विरागश्च कथं वदामि
स्वरूपनिर्वाणमनामयोऽहम ॥ १२ ॥

na cāsti deho na ca me videho
buddhir mano me na hi cendriyāṇi
rago virāgaś ca kathaṁ vadāmi
svarūpa-nirvāṇam anāmayo'ham.

12. I have no body or bodilessness, nor have I intelligence, mind, and senses. How shall I speak of attachment and detachment? I am free from disease—my form has been extinguished.

उल्लेखमात्रं न हि भिन्नमुच्चै-
रुल्लेखमात्रं न तिरोहितं वै ।
समासमं मित्र कथं वदामि
स्वरूपनिर्वाणमनामयोऽहम् ॥ १३ ॥

ullekha-mātraṁ na hi bhinnam uccaiḥ
ullekha-mātraṁ na tirohitaṁ vai
samāsamaṁ mitra kathaṁ vadāmi
svarūpa-nirvāṇam anāmayo'ham.

13. (The Self) is not separate or high and It has not disappeared even to the extent of allusion. Friend, how can I speak of It as identical or different? I am free from disease—my form has been extinguished.

Separate—from prakṛti or nature, according to Sāṁkhya philosophy.

High—beyond the relative world.

Disappeared—that is to say, when enveloped by māyā.

Identical—with the individual self or nature.

जितेन्द्रियोऽहं त्वजितेन्द्रियो वा
न संयमो मे नियमो न जातः ।
जयाजयौ मित्र कथं वदामि
स्वरूपनिर्वाणमनामयोऽहम् ॥ १४ ॥

jitendriyo'haṁ tu ajitendriyo vā
na saṁyamo me niyamo na jātaḥ
jayājayau mitra kathaṁ vadāmi
svarūpa-nirvāṇam anāmayo'ham.

14. Neither have I conquered the senses nor have I not conquered them. Self-restraint or discipline never occurred to me. Friend, how shall I speak of victory and defeat? I am free from disease—my form has been extinguished.

अमूर्तमूर्तिर्न च मे कदाचिदा-
द्यन्तमध्यं न च मे कदाचित् ।
बलाबलं मित्र कथं वदामि
स्वरूपनिर्वाणमनामयोऽहम् ॥ १५ ॥

amūrta-mūrtir na ca me kadācit
ādy-anta-madhyaṁ na ca me kadācit
balābalaṁ mitra kathaṁ vadāmi
svarūpa-nirvāṇam anāmayo'ham.

15. Never have I form or absence of form, never any beginning, middle, or end. Friend, how shall I speak of strength and weakness? I am free from disease—my form has been extinguished.

मृतामृतं वापि विषाविषं च
सञ्जायते तात न मे कदाचित् ।
अशुद्धशुद्धं च कथं वदामि
स्वरूपनिर्वाणमनामयोऽहम् ॥ १६ ॥

mṛtāmṛtaṁ vāpi viṣāviṣaṁ ca
sañjāyate tāta na me kadācit
aśuddha-śuddhaṁ ca kathaṁ vadāmi
svarūpa-nirvāṇam anāmayo'ham.

16. Never, my child, did I have death or deathlessness, poison or poisonlessness. How shall I speak of the pure and the impure? I am free from disease—my form has been extinguished.

Poison—the poison of māyā or ignorance.

स्वप्नः प्रबोधो न च योगमुद्रा
नक्तं दिवा वापि न मे कदाचित् ।
अतुर्यतुर्यं च कथं वदामि
स्वरूपनिर्वाणमनामयोऽहम् ॥ १७ ॥

svapnaḥ-prabodho na ca yoga-mudrā
naktaṁ divā vāpi na me kadācit
aturya-turyaṁ ca kathaṁ vadāmı
svarūpa-nirvāṇam anāmayo'ham.

17. Never have I sleep or awakening. Never do I practise concentration or hand-posture. For me there is neither day nor night. How shall I speak of the transcendental and relative states? I am free from disease—my form has been extinguished.

Hand-posture—practised as part of ceremonial worship.

Day, etc.—implying consciousness of time.

संविद्धि मां सर्वविसर्वमुक्तं
मायाविमाया न च मे कदाचित् ।
सन्ध्यादिकं कर्म कथं वदामि
स्वरूपनिर्वाणमनामयोऽहम् ॥ १८ ॥

samviddhi māṁ sarva-visarva-muktaṁ
māyā-vimāyā na ca me kadācit
sandhyādikaṁ karma kathaṁ vadāmi
svarūpa-nirvāṇam anāmayo'ham.

18. Know me as free from the all and from the details composing the all. I have neither illusion nor freedom from illusion. How shall I speak of such rituals as morning and evening devotions? I am free from disease—my form has been extinguished.

संविद्धि मां सर्वसमाधियुक्तं
संविद्धि मां लक्ष्यविलक्ष्यमुक्तम् ।
योगं वियोगं च कथं वदामि
स्वरूपनिर्वाणमनामयोऽहम् ॥ १९ ॥

saṁviddhi māṁ sarva-samādhi-yuktaṁ
saṁviddhi māṁ lakṣya-vilakṣya-muktam
yogaṁ viyogaṁ ca kathaṁ vadāmi
svarūpa-nirvāṇam anāmayo'ham.

19. Know me as endowed with all concentration. Know me as free from any relative or ultimate aim. How shall I speak of union and separation? I am free from disease—my form has been extinguished.

मूर्खोऽपि नाहं न च पण्डितोऽहं
मौनं विमौनं न च मे कदाचित् ।
तर्कं वितर्कं च कथं वदामि
स्वरूपनिर्वाणमनामयोऽहम् ॥ २० ॥

mūrkho'pi nāhaṁ na ca pandito'haṁ
maunaṁ vimaunaṁ na ca me kadācit
tarkaṁ vitarkaṁ ca kathaṁ vadāmi
svarūpa-nirvāṇam anāmayo'ham.

20. I am neither ignorant nor learned, I observe neither silence nor absence of silence. How shall I speak of argument and counter-argument? I am free from disease—my form has been extinguished.

पिता च माता च कुलं न जातिर्-
जन्मादि मृत्युर्न च मे कदाचित् ।
स्नेहं विमोहं च कथं वदामि
स्वरूपनिर्वाणमनामयोऽहम् ॥ २१ ॥

pitā ca mātā ca kulaṁ na jātiḥ
janmādi mṛtyur na ca me kadācit
snehaṁ vimohaṁ ca kathaṁ vadāmi
svarūpa-nirvāṇam anāmayo'ham.

21. Never do I have father, mother, family, caste, birth and death. How shall I speak of affection and infatuation? I am free from disease—my form has been extinguished.

अस्तं गतो नैव सदोदितोऽहं
तेजोवितेजो न च मे कदाचित् ।
सन्ध्यादिकं कर्म कथं वदामि
स्वरूपनिर्वाणमनामयोऽहम् ॥ २२ ॥

astaṁ gato naiva sadodito'haṁ
tejo-vitejo na ca me kadācit
sandhyādikaṁ karma kathaṁ vadāmi
svarūpa-nirvāṇam anāmayo'ham.

22. Never do I disappear—I am ever manifest. Never do I have effulgence or absence of effulgence. How shall I speak of such rituals as morning and evening devotions? I am free from disease—my form has been extinguished.

असंशयं विद्धि निराकुलं माम-
संशयं विद्धि निरन्तरं माम् ।
असंशयं विद्धि निरञ्जनं मां
स्वरूपनिर्वाणमनामयोऽहम् ॥ २३ ॥

asaṁśayaṁ viddhi nirākulaṁ māṁ
asaṁśayaṁ viddhi nirantaraṁ mām
asaṁśayaṁ viddhi nirañjanaṁ māṁ
svarūpa-nirvāṇam anāmayo'ham.

23. Know me beyond all doubt to be boundless. Know me beyond all doubt to be undivided. Know me beyond all doubt to be stainless. I am free from disease—my form has been extinguished.

ध्यानानि सर्वाणि परित्यजन्ति
शुभाशुभं कर्म परित्यजन्ति ।
त्यागामृतं तात पिबन्ति धीराः
स्वरूपनिर्वाणमनामयोऽहम् ॥ २४ ॥

dhyānāni sarvāṇi parityajanti
śubhāśubhaṁ karma parityajanti
tyagāmṛtaṁ tāta pibanti dhīrāḥ
svarūpa-nirvāṇam anāmayo'ham.

24. The wise, my child, give up all meditations; they give up all good and evil deeds and drink the nectar of renunciation. I am free from disease—my form has been extinguished.

विन्दति विन्दति न हि न हि यत्र
छन्दोलक्षणं न हि न हि तत्र ।
समरसमग्नो भावितपूतः
प्रलपति तत्त्वं परमवधूतः ॥ २५ ॥

vindati vindati na hi na hi yatra
chando-lakṣaṇaṁ na hi na hi tatra
samarasa-magno bhāvita-pūtaḥ
pralapati tattvaṁ param avadhūtaḥ.

25. There is verily no versification where one knows nothing. The supreme and free One, absorbed in the consciousness of the homogeneous Being and pure of thought, prattles about the Truth.

Versification—Dattātreya has been speaking in verse. But in the Transcendental, where there is neither knower or knowable, no speech—certainly no versification—is possible.

Prattles—The transcendental Reality cannot be adequately spoken of. Whatever Dattātreya has been saying about It can only be prattle.

Chapter V

ॐ इति गदितं गगनसमं तत्
न परापरसारविचार इति ।
अविलासविलासनिराकरणं
कथमक्षरबिन्दुसमुच्चरणम् ॥ १ ॥

Om iti gaditaṁ gagana-samaṁ tat
na parāpara-sāra-vicāra iti
avilāsa-vilāsa-nirākaraṇaṁ
katham akṣara-bindu-samuccaraṇam

1. The word Om is like the sky, it is not the discernment of the essence of high and low. How can there be enunciation of the point of the word (Om) which annuls the manifestation of the Unmanifest?

Like, etc.—The word Om is the same as God. Dattātreya describes Om to be "like the sky," inasmuch as the sky, like God, only seems to have colour and form, but is really formless.

Discernment, etc.—In the Absolute there is no distinction of high and low, good and evil, transcendental or relative.

Point, etc.—The word Om is so enunciated that the last letter, *m*, ends, as it were, in an inaudible sound.

This represents the transcendental aspect of reality and is called the "point" or bindu.

Annuls—Since the "point" of Om represents the Transcendental, its realization negates all relative realities.

इति तत्त्वमसिप्रभृतिश्रुतिभिः
प्रतिपादितमात्मनि तत्त्वमसि ।
त्वमुपाधिविवर्जितसर्वसमं
किमु रोदिषि मानसि सर्वसमम् ॥ २ ॥

iti tat tvam asi-prabhṛti-śrutibhiḥ
pratipāditam ātmani tat tvam asi
tvam upādhi-vivarjita-sarva-samaṁ
kimu rodiṣi mānasi sarva-samam.

2. The śrutis—such as "That thou art"—prove to thee thou art indeed That, devoid of adjuncts and the same in all. Why dost thou, who art the identity in all, grieve in thy heart?

Śrutis—the texts of the Vedas.

अधऊर्ध्वविवर्जितसर्वसमं
बहिरन्तरवर्जितसर्वसमम् ।
यदि चैकविवर्जितसर्वसमं
किमु रोदिषि मानसि सर्वसमम् ॥ ३ ॥

adha-ūrdhva-vivarjita-sarva-samaṁ
bahirantara-varjita-sarva-samam
yadi caikavivarjita-sarva-samaṁ
kimu rodiṣi mānasi sarva-samam.

3. If thou art the identity in all, if thou art devoid of above and below, within and without, and of even the sense of unity, then why dost thou, who art the identity in all, grieve in thy heart?

Above, etc.—transcendental and relative.

Sense, etc.—Not even unity may be spoken of the Self, since unity implies plurality.

न हि कल्पितकल्पविचार इति
न हि कारणकार्यविचार इति ।
पदसन्धिविवर्जितसर्वसमं
किमु रोदिषि मानसि सर्वसमम् ॥ ४ ॥

na hi kalpita-kalpa-vicāra iti
na hi kāraṇa-kārya-vicāra iti
pada-sandhi-vivarjita-sarva-samaṁ
kimu rodiṣi mānasi sarva-samam.

4. There is no discrimination of rules and precepts, there is no cause or effect. That which is the identity in all is without words and the collocation of words. Why dost thou, who art the identity in all, grieve in thy heart?

Without, etc.—The reference is to the doctrine that words are different aspects of God. But the word that is the absolute God has no components.

न हि बोधविबोधसमाधिरिति
न हि देशविदेशसमाधिरिति ।
न हि कालविकालसमाधिरिति
किमु रोदिषि मानसि सर्वसमम् ॥ ५ ॥

na hi bodha-vibodha-samādhir iti
na hi deśa-videśa-samādhir iti
na hi kāla-vikāla-samādhir iti
kimu rodiṣi mānasi sarva-samam.

5. There is no knowledge or ignorance and no practice of concentration. There is no space or absence of space and no practice of concentration. There is no time or absence of time and no practice of concentration. Why dost thou, who art the identity in all, grieve in thy heart?

No, etc.—Practice of concentration is undertaken to overcome ignorance and attain the knowledge of the Divine Self. But if the Self alone is, then there cannot be either ignorance or knowledge, or the need to practise concentration.

न हि कुम्भनभो न हि कुम्भ इति
न हि जीववपुर्न हि जीव इति ।
न हि कारणकार्यविभाग इति
किमु रोदिषि मानसि सर्वसमम् ॥ ६ ॥

na hi kuṁbha-nabho na hi kuṁbha iti
na hi jīva-vapur na hi jīva iti
na hi kāraṇa-kārya-vibhāga iti
kimu rodiṣi mānasi sarva-samam.

6. There is no pot-space or pot, no individual body or individual. There is no distinction of cause and effect. Why dost thou, who art the identity in all, grieve in thy heart?

Pot-space—the space within a pot, which is contrasted with the limitless space outside. Pot-space is possible only when there is a pot; similarly, individuality is possible only when there is a body. In the Self no such divisions exist.

इह सर्वनिरन्तरमोक्षपदं
लघुदीर्घविचारविहीन इति ।
न हि वर्तुलकोणविभाग इति
किमु रोदिषि मानसि सर्वसमम् ॥ ७ ॥

iha sarva-nirantara-mokṣa-padaṁ
laghu-dīrgha-vicāra-vihīna iti
na hi vartula-koṇa-vibhāga iti
kimu rodiṣi mānasi sarva-samam.

7. There is only the state of freedom which is the All and undifferentiated, which is devoid of the distinction of short and long, of round and angular. Why dost thou, who art the identity in all, grieve in thy heart?

इह शून्यविशून्यविहीन इति
इह शुद्धविशुद्धविहीन इति ।
इह सर्वविसर्वविहीन इति
किमु रोदिषि मानसि सर्वसमम् ॥ ८ ॥

iha śūnya-viśūnya-vihīna iti
iha śuddha-viśuddha-vihīna iti
iha sarva-visarva-vihīna iti
kimu rodiṣi mānasi sarva-samam.

8. Here is the One without void and absence of void, without purity and impurity, without the whole and the part. Why dost thou, who art the identity in all, grieve in thy heart?

न हि भिन्नविभिन्नविचार इति
बहिरन्तरसन्धिविचार इति ।
अरिमित्रविवर्जितसर्वसमं
किमु रोदिषि मानसि सर्वसमम् ॥ ९ ॥

na hi bhinna-vibhinna-vicāra iti
bahir-antara-sandhi-vicāra iti
ari-mitra-vivarjita-sarva-samaṁ
kimu rodiṣi mānasi sarva-samam.

9. There is no distinction of the different and nondifferent. There is no distinction of within, without, or junction of the two. It is the same in all, devoid of friend and foe. Why dost thou, who art the identity in all, grieve in thy heart?

Different—differentiated reality.

Nondifferent—undifferentiated Reality.

न हि शिष्यविशिष्यस्वरूप इति
न चराचरभेदविचार इति ।
इह सर्वनिरन्तरमोक्षपदं
किमु रोदिषि मानसि सर्वसमम् ॥ १० ॥

na hi śiṣya-viśiṣya-svarūpa iti
na carācara-bheda-vicāra iti
iha sarva-nirantara-mokṣa-padaṁ
kimu rodiṣi mānasi sarva-samam.

10. It is not of the nature of disciple or non-disciple; nor is it the discernment of the differ-

ence between the living and the nonliving. There is only the state of freedom—the All, the Undifferentiated. Why dost thou, who art the identity in all, grieve in thy heart?

ननु रूपविरूपविहीन इति
ननु भिन्नविभिन्नविहीन इति ।
ननु सर्गविसर्गविहीन इति
किमु रोदिषि मानसि सर्वसमम् ॥ ११ ॥

nanu rūpa-virūpa-vihīna iti
nanu bhinna-vibhinna-vihīna iti
nanu sarga-visarga-vihīna iti
kimu rodiṣi mānasi sarva-samam.

11. It is without form and formlessness. It is without difference and nondifference. It is without manifestation and evolution. Why dost thou, who art the identity in all, grieve in thy heart?

न गुणागुणपाशनिबन्ध इति
मृतजीवनकर्म करोमि कथम् ।
इति शुद्धनिरञ्जनसर्वसमं
किमु रोदिषि मानसि सर्वसमम् ॥ १२ ॥

na guṇāguṇa-pāśa-nibandha iti
mṛta-jīvana-karma karomi katham
iti śuddha-nirañjana-sarva-samaṁ
kimu rodiṣi mānasi sarva-samam.

12. There is no bondage due to fetters of good and evil qualities. How shall I perform the actions related to death and life? There is only the pure, stainless Being—the same in all. Why dost thou, who art the identity in all, grieve in thy heart?

Good,etc.—The good and evil qualities which make up our relative individuality result from experiences of past births. The soul has no quality or karma, as it is timeless.

Perform, etc.—In Self-knowledge there is no consciousness of life or death.

इह भावविभावविहीन इति
इह कामविकामविहीन इति ।
इह बोधतमं खलु मोक्षसमं
किमु रोदिषि मानसि सर्वसमम् ।। १३ ।।

iha bhāva-vibhāva-vihīna iti
iha kāma-vikāma-vihīna iti
iha bodhatamaṁ khalu mokṣa-samaṁ
kimu rodiṣi mānasi sarva-samam.

13. Here is the Being devoid of existence and nonexistence, of desire and desirelessness. Here verily is the highest Consciousness, identical with freedom. Why dost thou, who art the identity in all, grieve in thy heart?

इह तत्त्वनिरन्तरतत्त्वमिति
न हि सन्धिविसन्धिविहीन इति ।
यदि सर्वविवर्जितसर्वसमं
किमु रोदिषि मानसि सर्वसमम् ॥ १४ ॥

iha tattva-nirantara-tattvam iti
na hi sandhi-visandhi-vihīna iti
yadi sarva-vivarjita-sarva-samaṁ
kimu rodiṣi mānasi sarva-samam.

14. Here is the Truth undifferentiated by truths, devoid of junction and disjunction. Since it is the same in all and devoid of all, why dost thou, who art the identity in all, grieve in thy heart?

Undifferentiated, etc.—not containing lesser, relative truths.

Junction, etc.—of puruṣa and prakṛti, soul and matter.

Devoid—The Self is not the aggregate of any or all realities.

अनिकेतकुटी परिवारसमं
इह सङ्गविसङ्गविहीनपरम् ।
इह बोधविबोधविहीनपरं
किमु रोदिषि मानसि सर्वसमम् ॥ १५ ॥

aniketa-kuṭī-parivāra-samaṁ
iha saṅga-visaṅga-vihīna-param
iha bodha-vibodha-vihīna-paraṁ
kimu rodiṣi mānasi sarva-samam.

15. Here is the Supreme, devoid of association and dissociation, unlike a house, cottage, or sheath. Here is the Supreme devoid of knowledge and ignorance. Why dost thou, who art the identity in all, grieve in thy heart?

Unlike, etc.—The Self is not the receptacle in which the infinite realities of the universe are contained, as a house, cottage, or sheath holds objects within it.

अविकारविकारमसत्यमिति
अविलक्षविलक्षमसत्यमिति ।
यदि केवलमात्मनि सत्यमिति
किमु रोदिषि मानसि सर्वसमम् ॥ १६ ॥

avikāra-vikāram asatyam iti
avilakṣa-vilakṣam asatyam iti
yadi kevalam ātmani satyam iti
kimu rodiṣi mānasi sarva-samam.

16. Change and changelessness, the definable and the indefinable are untrue. If the truth is in the Self alone, why dost thou, who art the identity in all, grieve in thy heart?

इह सर्वसमं खलु जीव इति
इह सर्वनिरन्तरजीव इति ।
इह केवलनिश्चलजीव इति
किमु रोदिषि मानसि सर्वसमम् ॥ १७ ॥

iha sarva-samaṁ khalu jīva iti
iha sarva-nirantara-jīva iti
iha kevala-niścala-jīva iti
kimu rodiṣi mānasi sarva-samam.

17. Here verily is the conscious Being who is completely the All. Here is the conscious Being who is all-comprehensive and undivided. Here is the conscious Being, alone and immutable. Why dost thou, who art the identity in all, grieve in thy heart?

अविवेकविवेकमबोध इति
अविकल्पविकल्पमबोध इति ।
यदि चैकनिरन्तरबोध इति
किमु रोदिषि मानसि सर्वसमम् ॥ १८ ॥

aviveka-vivekam abodha iti
avikalpa-vikalpam abodha iti
yadi caikanirantara-bodha iti
kimu rodiṣi mānasi sarva-samam.

18. It is ignorance to see difference in the Undifferentiated. Doubt in what is beyond doubt is ignorance. If there is only the one undivided Consciousness, then why dost thou, who art the identity in all, grieve in thy heart?

न हि मोक्षपदं न हि बन्धपदं
न हि पुण्यपदं न हि पापपदम् ।
न हि पर्णपदं न हि रिक्तपदं
किमु रोदिषि मानसि सर्वसमम् ॥ १९ ॥

na hi mokṣa-padaṁ na hi bandha-padaṁ
na hi puṇya-padaṁ na hi pāpa-padam
na hi pūrṇa-padaṁ na hi rikta-padaṁ
kimu rodiṣi mānasi sarva-samam.

19. There is no state of liberation, no state of bondage, no state of virtue, no state of vice. There is no state of perfection and no state of destitution. Why dost thou, who art the identity in all, grieve in thy heart?

यदि वर्णविवर्णविहीनसमं
यदि कारणकार्यविहीनसमम् ।
यदि भेदविभेदविहीनसमं
किमु रोदिषि मानसि सर्वसमम् ॥ २० ॥

yadi varṇa-vivarṇa-vihīna-samaṁ
yadi kāraṇa-kārya-vihīna-samam
yadi bheda-vibheda-vihīna-samaṁ
kimu rodiṣi mānasi sarva-samam.

20. If the homogeneous Being is devoid of cause and effect, division and subdivision colour and lack of colour, then why dost thou, who art the identity in all, grieve in thy heart?

इह सर्वनिरन्तरसर्वचिते
इह केवलनिश्चलसर्वचिते ।
द्विपदादिविवर्जितसर्वचिते
किमु रोदिषि मानसि सर्वसमम् ॥ २१ ॥

iha sarva-nirantara-sarva-cite
iha kevala-niścala-sarva-cite
dvipadādi-vivarjita-sarva-cite
kimu rodiṣi mānasi sarva-samam.

21. The Self is here in the universal Consciousness which is the All and undivided. It is here in the universal Consciousness which is

absolute and immovable. It is here in the universal Consciousness which is devoid of men and other beings. Why dost thou, who art the identity in all, grieve in thy heart?

अतिसर्वनिरन्तरसर्वगतं
अतिनिर्मलनिश्चलसर्वगतम् ।
दिनरात्रिविवर्जितसर्वगतं
किमु रोदिषि मानसि सर्वसमम् ॥ २२ ॥

ati sarva-nirantara-sarva-gataṁ
ati-nirmala-niścala-sarva-gatam
dina-rātri-vivarjita-sarva-gataṁ
kimu rodiṣi mānasi sarva-samam.

22. The Self transcends all, is indivisible and all-pervading. It is free from stain of attachment, immovable and all-pervading. It is without day and night and all-pervading. Why dost thou, who art the identity in all, grieve in thy heart?

न हि बन्धविबन्धसमागमनं
न हि योगवियोगसमागमनम् ।
न हि तर्कवितर्कसमागमनं
किमु रोदिषि मानसि सर्वसमम् ॥ २३ ॥

na hi bandha- vibandha-samāgamanaṁ
na hi yoga-viyoga-samāgamanam
na hi tarka-vitarka-samāgamanaṁ
kimu rodiṣi mānasi sarva-samam.

23. There is no coming of bondage and freedom from bondage. There is no coming of union and separation. There is no coming of reasoning and disputation. Why dost thou, who art the identity in all, grieve in thy heart?

इह कालविकालनिराकरणं
अणुमात्रकृशानुनिराकरणम् ।
न हि केवलसत्यनिराकरणं
किमु रोदिषि मानसि सर्वसमम् ॥ २४ ॥

iha kāla-vikāla-nirākaraṇaṁ
aṇu-mātra kṛśānu-nirākaraṇam
na hi kevala-satya-nirākaraṇaṁ
kimu rodiṣi mānasi sarva-samam.

24. Here is the negation of time, untime, and even the atom of fire, but no negation of the absolute Truth. Why dost thou, who art the identity in all, grieve in thy heart?

Atom,etc.—"Fire" is one of the five original elements of which the phenomenal universe is made. Here fire stands for all the five elements. (*See Chapter one*, *verse* 3.)

इह देहविदेहविहीन इति
ननु स्वप्नसुषुप्तिविहीनपरम् ।
अभिधानविधानविहीनपरं
किमु रोदिषि मानसि सर्वसमम् ॥ २५ ॥

iha deha-videha-vihīna iti
nanu svapna-suṣupti-vihīna-param
abhidhāna-vidhāna-vihīna-paraṁ
kimu rodiṣi mānasi sarva-samam.

25. Here is the Self devoid of body and disembodiment. Here verily is the supreme One devoid of dream and deep sleep. Here is the supreme One devoid of name and injunctions. Why dost thou, who art the identity in all, grieve in thy heart?

गगनोपमशुद्धविशालसमं
अतिसर्वविवर्जितसर्वसमम् ।
गतसारविसारविकारसमं
किमु रोदिषि मानसि सर्वसमम् ॥ २६ ॥

gaganopama-śuddha-viśāla-samaṁ
ati sarva-vivarjita-sarva-samam
gata-sāra-visāra-vikāra-samaṁ
kimu rodiṣi mānasi sarva-samam.

26. Pure, vast and homogeneous like the sky, the Self is the same in all and devoid of all. It

is the homogeneous Being divested of essence, nonessence, and change. Why dost thou, who art the identity in all, grieve in thy heart?

इह धर्मविधर्मविरागतर-
मिह वस्तुविवस्तुविरागतरम् ।
इह कामविकामविरागतरं
किमु रोदिषि मानसि सर्वसमम् ॥ २७ ॥

iha dharma-vidharma-virāga taraṁ
iha vastu-vivastu-virāga taram
iha kāma-vikāma-virāga taraṁ
kimu rodiṣi mānasi sarva-samam.

27. Here is the Self, which is more than dispassionate to virtue and vice, to substance and nonsubstance, to desire and desirelessness. Why dost thou, who art the identity in all, grieve in thy heart?

सुखदुःखविवर्जितसर्वसम-
मिह शोकविशोकविहीनपरम् ।
गुरुशिष्यविवर्जिततत्त्वपरं
किमु रोदिषि मानस सर्वसमम् ॥ २८ ॥

sukha-duḥkha-vivarjita-sarva-samaṁ
iha śoka-viśoka-vihīna-param
guru-śiṣya-vivarjita-tattva-paraṁ
kimu rodiṣi mānasi sarva-samam.

28. Here is the Self, the same in all, which is without grief and grieflessness. Here is the Supreme, without happiness and sorrow. The supreme Truth is devoid of teacher and disciple. Why dost thou, who art the identity in all, grieve in thy heart?

न किलाङ्कुरसारविसार इति
न चलाचलसाम्यविसाम्यमिति ।
अविचारविचारविहीनमिति
किमु रोदिषि मानसि सर्वसमम् ॥ २९ ॥

na kilāṅkura-sāra-visāra iti
na calācala-sāmya-visāmyam iti
avicāra-vicāra-vihīnam iti
kimu rodiṣi mānasi sarva-samam.

29. Verily there is no offshoot, essence, or absence of essence. Neither is there the movable nor the immovable, sameness nor variety. The Self is devoid of reason and unreason. Why dost thou, who art the identity in all, grieve in thy heart?

इह सारसमुच्चयसारमिति
कथितं निजभावविभेद इति ।
विषये करणत्वमसत्यमिति
किमु रोदिषि मानसि सर्वसमम् ॥ ३० ॥

iha sāra-samuccaya-sāraṁ iti
kathitaṁ nijabhāva-vibheda iti
viṣaye karaṇatvam asatyam iti
kimu rodiṣi mānasi sarva-samam.

30. Here is the Essence, the concentration of all essences, which is said to be different from one's individual consciousness. To be the instrument of the perception of objects is unreal. Why dost thou, who art the identity in all, grieve in thy heart?

Instrument, etc.—The Self or pure Consciousness is absolute and has nothing to do with any object.

बहुधा श्रुतयः प्रवदन्ति यतो
वियदादिरिदं मृगतोयसमम् ।
यदि चैकनिरन्तरसर्वसमं
किमु रोदिषि मानसि सर्वसमम् ॥ ३१ ॥

bahudhā śrutayaḥ pravadanti yato
viyadādir idaṁ mṛga-toya-samam
yadi caikanirantara-sarva-samaṁ
kimu rodiṣi mānasi sarva-samam.

31. Since the Vedas have declared variously that this (universe) made of ether and the like is like a mirage, and since the Self is one, indivisible, and the same in all, why dost thou, who art the identity in all, grieve in thy heart?

विन्दति विन्दति न हि न हि यत्र
छन्दोलक्षणं न हि न हि तत्र ।
समरसमग्नो भावितपूतः
प्रलपति तत्त्वं परमवधूतः ॥ ३२ ॥

vindati vindati na hi na hi yatra
chando-lakṣaṇaṁ na hi na hi tatra
samarasa-magno bhāvita-pūtaḥ
pralapati tattvaṁ param avadhūtaḥ.

32. Where one knows nothing, there is verily no versification. The supreme and free One, pure of thought, absorbed in the consciousness of the homogeneous Being, prattles about the Truth.

Prattles—The highest Truth cannot be expressed. Whatever is said about It is at least partly nonsensical.

CHAPTER VI

बहुधा श्रुतयः प्रवदन्ति वयं
वियदादिरिदं मृगतोयसमम् ।
यदि चैकनिरन्तरसर्वशिव
मुपमेयमथोह्युपमा च कथम् ॥ १ ॥

bahudhā śrutayaḥ pravadanti vayaṁ
viyadādir idaṁ mṛga-toya-samam
yadi caika-nirantara-sarva-śivam
upameyam atho hyupamā ca katham?

1. The srutis declare in various ways that all this, the ether and its like, and we ourselves, are like a mirage. If there is only one indivisible, all-comprehensive Absolute, how can there be the comparable and the comparison?

All,etc.—the visible and the invisible worlds.

अविभक्तिविभक्तिविहीनपरं
ननु कार्यविकार्यविहीनपरम् ।
यदि चैकनिरन्तरसर्वशिवं
यजनं च कथं तपनं च कथम् ॥ २ ॥

avibhakti-vibhakti-vihīna-paraṁ
nanu kārya-vikārya vihīna-param

yadi caika-nirantara-sarva-śivaṁ
yajanaṁ ca kathaṁ tapanaṁ ca katham.

2. The Supreme is without divisibility and indivisibility. The Supreme is without activity and changeability. If there is only one indivisible, all-comprehensive Absolute, how can there be worship, how can there be austerity?

How,etc.—Worship and austerity imply recognition of many existences and are therefore unreal.

मन एव निरन्तरसर्वगतं
ह्यविशालविशालविहीनपरम् ।
मन एव निरन्तरसर्वशिवं
मनसापि कथं वचसा च कथम् ॥ ३ ॥

mana eva nirantara-sarva-gataṁ
hyaviśāla-viśāla-vihīna-param
mana eva nirantara-sarva-śivaṁ
manasāpi kathaṁ vacasā ca katham.

3. The Mind is verily supreme, undivided, all-pervasive, and devoid of largeness and smallness. The Mind is indeed the indivisible, all-comprehensive Absolute. How can we do anything with the mind and speech?

Mind—used as a synonym of Self.

Mind—used in its usual sense.

दिनरात्रिविभेदनिराकरण-
मुदितानुदितस्य निराकरणम् ।
यदि चैकनिरन्तरसर्वंशिवं
रविचन्द्रमसौ ज्वलनश्च कथम् ॥ ४ ॥

dina-rātri-vibheda-nirākaraṇam
uditānuditasya-nirākaraṇam
yadi caika-nirantara-sarva-śivaṁ
ravi-candramasau jvalanaś ca katham.

4. The Self is the negation of the distinction between day and night. The Self is the negation of the risen and not-risen. If there is only one indivisible, all-comprehensive Absolute, how can there be the sun, the moon, and fire?

Risen, etc.—become manifest. Manifestation and its opposite are both parts of phenomenal existence and cannot be true of the absolute Self.

गतकामविकामविभेद इति
गतचेष्टविचेष्टविभेद इति ।
यदि चैकनिरन्तरसर्वंशिवं
बहिरन्तरभिन्नमतिश्च कथम् ॥ ५ ॥

gata-kāma-vikāma vibheda iti
gata-ceṣṭa-viceṣṭa-vibheda iti
yadi caika-nirantara-sarva-śivaṁ
bahir-antara-bhinna-matiś ca katham.

5. The Self is that from which the distinctions of desire and desirelessness, of action and

inaction are gone. If there is only one indivisible, all-comprehensive Absolute, how can there be consciousness differentiated by exterior and interior?

यदि सारविसारविहीन इति
यदि शून्यविशून्यविहीन इति ।
यदि चैकनिरन्तरसर्वशिवं
प्रथमं च कथं चरमं च कथम् ॥ ६ ॥

yadi sāra-visāra-vihīna iti
yadi śūnya-viśūnya-vihīna iti
yadi caika-nirantara-sarva-śivaṁ
prathamaṁ ca kathaṁ caramaṁ ca katham.

6. If the Self is devoid of essence and lack of essence, if it is without void and nonvoid, if there is only one indivisible, all-comprehensive Absolute, how can there be a first, how can there be a last?

Essence, etc.—substance from which the universe originates. "Lack of essence" means lack of such creative substance. Both these terms are inapplicable to the Absolute Brahman.

First—origination of the universe or the waking state.

Last—dissolution of the universe or deep sleep state.

यदि भेदविभेदनिराकरणं
यदि वेदकवेद्यनिराकरणम् ।

यदि चैकनिरन्तरसर्वशिवं
तृतीयं च कथं तुरीयं च कथम् ॥ ७ ॥

yadi bheda-vibheda-nirākaraṇaṁ
yadi vedaka-vedya-nirākaraṇam
yadi caika-nirantara-sarva-śivaṁ
tritīyaṁ ca kathaṁ turīyaṁ ca katham.

7. If the Self is the negation of difference and nondifference, if it is the negation of knower and knowable, if there is only one indivisible, all-comprehensive Absolute, how can there be the third, how can there be the fourth?

Third—deep sleep state.

Fourth—the transcendental state. But the term "fourth" implies relativity.

गदिताविदितं न हि सत्यमिति
विदिताविदितं न हि सत्यमिति ।
यदि चैकनिरन्तरसर्वशिवं
विषयेन्द्रियबुद्धिमनांसि कथम् ॥ ८ ॥

gaditāviditaṁ na hi satyam iti
viditāviditaṁ na hi satyam iti
yadi caikanirantara-sarva-śivaṁ
viṣayendriya-buddhi-manāṁsi katham.

8. The spoken and the unspoken are not the Truth, the known and the unknown are not

the Truth. If there is only one indivisible, all-comprehensive Absolute, how can there be objects, senses, mind, and intellect?

Spoken—that which is expressed.

Unspoken—that which has not been expressed. The unspoken also is relative, being the opposite of the spoken, and is therefore not the Truth.

गगनं पवनो न हि सत्यमिति
धरणी दहनो न हि सत्यमिति ।
यदि चैकनिरन्तरसर्वशिवं
जलदश्च कथं सलिलं च कथम् ॥ ९ ॥

gaganaṁ pavano na hi satyam iti
dharaṇī-dahano na hi satyam iti
yadi caika-nirantara-sarva-śivaṁ
jaladaś ca kathaṁ salilaṁ ca katham.

9. Ether and air are not the Truth; earth and fire are not the Truth. If there is only one indivisible, all-comprehensive Absolute, how can there be cloud, how can there be water?

Cloud,etc.—"Cloud" and "water" can also be understood figuratively, meaning the original cause of the universe and manifold phenomena.

यदि कल्पितलोकनिराकरणं
यदि कल्पितदेवनिराकरणम् ।

यदि चैकनिरन्तरसर्वशिवं
गुणदोषविचारमतिश्च कथम् ॥ १० ॥

yadi kalpita-loka-nirākaraṇaṁ
yadi kalpita-deva-nirākaraṇam
yadi caika-nirantara-sarva-śivaṁ
guṇa-doṣa-vicāra-matiś ca katham.

10. If the Self is the negation of imagined worlds, if It is the negation of imagined gods, if there is only one indivisible, all-comprehensive Absolute, how can there be discriminating consciousness of good and evil?

Imagined—because not absolutely real.

मरणामरणं हि निराकरणं
करणाकरणं हि निराकरणम् ।
यदि चैकनिरन्तरसर्वशिवं
गमनागमनं हि कथं वदति ॥ ११ ॥

maraṇāmaraṇam hi nirākaraṇaṁ
karaṇākaraṇaṁ hi nirākaraṇam
yadi caika-nirantara-sarva-śivaṁ
gamanāgamanaṁ hi kathaṁ vadati.

11. The Self is the negation of death and deathlessness. It is the negation of action and inaction. If there is only one indivisible, all-

comprehensive Absolute, how can one speak of coming and going?

Coming,etc.—birth and death.

प्रकृतिः पुरुषो न हि भेद इति
न हि कारणकार्यविभेद इति ।
यदि चैकनिरन्तरसर्वशिवं
पुरुषापुरुषं च कथं वदति ॥ १२ ॥

prakṛtiḥ puruṣo na hi bheda iti
na hi kāraṇa-kārya-vibheda iti
yadi caika-nirantara-sarva-śivaṁ
puruṣāpuruṣaṁ ca kathaṁ vadati.

12. No such distinctions exist as prakṛti and puruṣa. There is no difference between cause and effect. If there is only one indivisible, all-comprehensive Absolute, how can one speak of self and not-self?

तृतीयं न हि दुःखसमागमनं
न गुणाद्द्वितीयस्य समागमनम् ।
यदि चैकनिरन्तरसर्वशिवं
स्थविरश्च युवा च शिशुश्च कथम् ॥ १३ ॥

tṛtīyaṁ na hi duḥkha-samāgamanaṁ
na guṇād dvitīyasya samāgamanam
yadi caika-nirantara-sarva-śivaṁ
sthaviraś ca yuvā ca śiśuś ca katham.

13. There is no coming of the third kind of misery or of the second kind of misery, due to the guṇas. If there is only one indivisible, all-comprehensive Absolute, how can there be an old man, a young man, or an infant?

Third, etc.—Indian philosophies usually speak of three kinds of misery; first, that arising from one's own self; second, that originating from other beings and things; and third, that arising from superhuman sources. Although the first kind of misery is not mentioned in the text, all three are meant and all arise from nature or prakṛti which is composed of three guṇas.

ननु आश्रमवर्णविहीनपरं
ननु कारणकर्तृविहीनपरम् ।
यदि चैकनिरन्तरसर्वशिव-
मविनष्टविनष्टमतिश्च कथम् ॥ १४ ॥

nanu āśrama-varna-vihīna-paraṁ
nanu kārana-kartṛ-vihīna-param
yadi caika-nirantara-sarva-śivaṁ
avinaṣṭa-vinaṣṭa-matiś ca katham.

14. The Supreme is without caste and stage of life, without cause and agent. If there is only one indivisible, all-comprehensive Absolute, how can there be consciousness of the destroyed and the undestroyed?

Caste, etc.—The Hindus recognize four castes (representing the priestly, military, trading, and labouring classes) and four stages of life (those of the student, householder, contemplative, and monk). These have nothing to do with the Self, which is identical with the Supreme.

Cause, etc.—The Self has neither any material cause nor any efficient cause (agent). Also it may mean that the Self is not the cause or the doer of anything.

Destroyed, etc.—By "the destroyed" is meant the world of phenomena which disappears at the attainment of Knowledge, and by "the undestroyed" is meant the eternal Self. But the dual consciousness of the eternal Self and phenomena is impossible in the Absolute.

ग्रसिताग्रसितं च वितथ्यमिति
जनिताजनितं च वितथ्यमिति ।
यदि चैकनिरन्तरसर्वशिव-
मविनाशि विनाशि कथं हि भवेत् ॥ १५ ॥

grasitāgrasitaṁ ca vitathyam iti
janitājanitaṁ ca vitathyam iti
yadi caika-nirantara-sarva-śivaṁ
avināśi vināśi kathaṁ hi bhavet.

15. The destroyed and the undestroyed are both false. The born and the unborn are both false. If there is only one indivisible, all-comprehensive Absolute, how can there be the perishable and the imperishable?

पुरुषापुरुषस्य विनष्टमिति
वनितावनितस्य विनष्टमिति ।
यदि चैकनिरन्तरसर्वशिव-
मविनोदविनोदमतिश्च कथम् ॥ १६ ॥

puruṣāpuruṣasya vinaṣṭam iti
vanitāvanitasya vinaṣṭam iti
yadi caika-nirantara-sarva-śivaṁ
avinoda-vinoda-matiś ca katham.

16. The Self is the annihilation of the masculine and the nonmasculine. It is the annihilation of the feminine and the nonfeminine. If there is only one indivisible, all-comprehensive Absolute, how can there be consciousness of joy and lack of joy?

Annihilation—that is, the Self is the negation of etc.

Masculine, etc.—There is no sex in the Self. The words "masculine" and "feminine" may also mean puruṣa (soul) and prakṛti (nature).

यदि मोहविषादविहीनपरो
यदि संशयशोकविहीनपरः ।
यदि चैकनिरन्तरसर्वशिव-
महमेति ममेति कथं च पुनः ॥ १७ ॥

yadi moha-viṣāda-vihīna paro
yadi saṁśaya-śoka-vihīna paraḥ

yadi caika-nirantara-sarva-śivaṁ
aham eti mameti kathaṁ ca punaḥ.

17. If the Supreme is free of delusion and sorrow, doubt and grief, if there is only one indivisible, all-comprehensive Absolute, how can there be "I" and "mine"?

ननु धर्मविधर्मविनाश इति
ननु बन्धविबन्धविनाश इति ।
यदि चैकनिरन्तरसर्वशिव
मिहदु:खविदु:खमतिश्च कथम् ॥ १८ ॥

nanu dharma-vidharma-vināśa iti
nanu bandha-vibandha-vināśa iti
yadi caika-nirantara-sarva-śivaṁ
iha duḥkha-viduḥkha-matiś ca katham.

18. The Supreme is the destruction of virtue and vice. It is the destruction of bondage and freedom from bondage. If there is only one indivisible, all-comprehensive Absolute, how can there be here any consciousness of sorrow and absence of sorrow?

न हि याज्ञिकयज्ञविभाग इति
न हुताशनवस्तुविभाग इति ।
यदि चैकनिरन्तरसर्वशिवं
वद कर्मफलानि भवन्ति कथम् ॥ १९ ॥

na hi yājñika-yajna-vibhāga iti
na hutāśana-vastu-vibhāga iti
yadi caika-nirantara-sarva-śivaṁ
vada karma-phalāni bhavanti katham.

19. No distinction of sacrificer and sacrifice exists. No distinction of fire and ingredients exists. If there is only one indivisible, all-comprehensive Absolute, say how there can be any fruits of work.

Sacrificer, etc.—The reference is to the fire ritual in which priests make oblations into the sacred fire for attainment of earthly or heavenly ends. Such a ritual has nothing to do with the supreme Self.

ननु शोकविशोकविमुक्त इति
ननु दर्पविदर्पविमुक्त इति ।
यदि चैकनिरन्तरसर्वशिवं
ननु रागविरागमतिश्च कथम् ॥ २० ॥

nanu śoka-viśoka-vimukta iti
nanu darpa-vidarpa-vimukta iti
yadi caika-nirantara-sarva-śivaṁ
nanu rāga-virāga-matiś ca katham.

20. The Self is verily free from sorrow and absence of sorrow. The Self is free from pride and absence of pride. If there is only one indivisible, all-comprehensive Absolute, how can

there be consciousness of attachment and non-attachment?

न हि मोहविमोहविकार इति
न हि लोभविलोभविकार इति ।
यदि चैकनिरन्तरसर्वशिवं
ह्यविवेकविवेकमतिश्च कथम् ॥ २१ ॥

na hi moha-vimoha-vikāra iti
na hi lobha-vilobha-vikāra iti
yadi caika-nirantara-sarva-śivaṁ
hyaviveka-viveka-matiś ca katham.

21. No such change as illusion and freedom from illusion exists. No such change as greed and freedom from greed exists. If there is only one indivisible, all-comprehensive Absolute, how can there be consciousness of discrimination and lack of discrimination?

Discrimination—between the Real and the unreal.

त्वमहं न हि हन्त कदाचिदपि
कुलजातिविचारमसत्यमिति ।
अहमेव शिवः परमार्थ इति
अभिवादनमत्र करोमि कथम् ॥ २२ ॥

tvam ahaṁ na hi hanta kadācid api
kula-jāti-vicāram asatyam iti

aham eva śivaḥ paramārtha iti
abhivādanam atra karomi katham.

22. There are never any 'you' and 'I' The discrimination of family and race is false. I am indeed the Absolute and the supreme Truth. In that case how can I make any salutation?

Salutation—Salutation implies at least duality.

गुरुशिष्यविचारविशीर्णं इति
उपदेशविचारविशीर्णं इति ।
अहमेव शिवः परमार्थ इति
अभिवादनमत्र करोमि कथम् ॥ २३ ॥

guru-śisya-vicāra-viśīrṇa iti
upadeśa vicāra-viśīrṇa iti
aham eva śivaḥ paramārtha iti
abhivādanam atra karomi katham.

23. The Self is that in which the distinction of teacher and disciple disappears and in which the consideration of instruction also disappears. I am indeed the Absolute and the supreme Truth. How can I, in that case, make any salutation?

न हि कल्पितदेहविभाग इति
न हि कल्पितलोकविभाग इति ।

अहमेव शिवः परमार्थ इति
अभिवादनमत्र करोमि कथम् ॥ २४ ॥

na hi kalpita-deha-vibhāga iti
na hi kalpita-loka-vibhāga iti
aham eva śivaḥ paramārtha iti
abhivādanam atra karomi katham.

24. There is no imagined division of bodies. There is no imagined division of worlds. I am indeed the Absolute and the supreme Truth. In that case how can I make any salutation?

Bodies—The soul in the state of ignorance is considered to be endowed with three bodies—gross, subtle, and causal. Also the bodies of the different kinds of beings, natural and supernatural, may be meant.

सरजो विरजो न कदाचिदपि
ननु निर्मलनिश्चलशुद्ध इति ।
अहमेव शिवः परमार्थ इति
अभिवादनमत्र करोमि कथम् ॥ २५ ॥

sarajo virajo na kadācid api
nanu nirmala-niścala-śuddha iti
aham eva śivaḥ paramārtha iti
abhivādanam atra karomi katham.

25. The Self, never endowed with passion or devoid of it, is verily spotless, immovable and

pure. I am indeed the Absolute and the supreme Truth. In that case how can I make any salutation?

न हि देहविदेहविकल्प इति
अनृतं चरितं न हि सत्यमिति।
अहमेव शिवः परमार्थ इनि
अभिवादनमत्र करोमि कथम् ॥ २६ ॥

na hi deha-videha-vikalpa iti
anṛtaṁ caritaṁ na hi satyam iti
aham eva śivaḥ paramārtha iti
abhivādanam atra karomi katham.

26. No distinction such as body and bodilessness exists, nor is it true that there is false action. I am indeed the Absolute and the supreme Truth. In that case how can I make any salutation?

True, etc.—To think that false action (such as false perception, illusion, or any action pertaining to relative life) exists, is possible only in relative existence and ignorance. Such a conclusion, therefore, is false.

विन्दति विन्दति न हि न हि यत्र
छन्दोलक्षणं न हि न हि तत्र ।
समरसमग्नो भावितपूतः
प्रलपति तत्त्वं परमवधूतः ॥ २७ ॥

vindati vindati nahi nahi yatra
chando-lakṣaṇaṁ nahi nahi tatra
samarasa-magno bhāvita-pūtaḥ
pralapati tattvaṁ param avadhūtaḥ.

27. Where one knows nothing, there is verily no versification. The supreme and free One, pure of thought, absorbed in the consciousness of the homogeneous Being, prattles about the Truth.

Chapter VII

रथ्याकर्पटविरचितकन्थः
पुण्यापुण्यविवर्जितपन्थः ।
शून्यागारे तिष्ठति नग्नो
शुद्धनिरञ्जनसमरसमग्नः ॥ १ ॥

rathyā-karpaṭa-viracita-kanthaḥ
puṇyāpuṇya-vivarjita-panthaḥ
śūnyāgāre tiṣṭhati nagno
śuddha-nirañjana-samarasa-magnaḥ.

1. The enlightened one, nude or clad in a patched garment made of rags gathered from roads, follows the path which is devoid of virtue and vice and stays in an empty abode, absorbed in the pure, stainless, homogeneous Being.

Devoid, etc.—because he now realizes he is the transcendental, absolute Being, beyond all rules and actions of relative life.

Stainless—free from all adjuncts that make the Self appear as limited, ignorant, and impure.

लक्ष्यालक्ष्यविवर्जितलक्ष्यो
युक्तायुक्तविवर्जितदक्षः ।
केवलतत्त्वनिरञ्जनपूतो
वादविवादः कथमवधूतः ॥ २ ॥

lakṣyālakṣya-vivarjita-lakṣyo
yuktāyukta-vivarjita dakṣaḥ
kevala-tattva-nirañjana-pūtaḥ
vādavivādaḥ katham avadhūtaḥ.

2. The enlightened one aims at that which is without any mark or marklessness. He is skilful, being devoid of right and wrong. He is the absolute Truth, stainless and pure. How can the liberated one engage in discussion and disputation?

Mark , etc.—"Mark" means defining attribute. "Marklessness" is absence of attributes. But even absence of attributes cannot be imputed to the transcendental Self, since the absence of attributes implies the existence of attributes.

Engage,etc.—Discussion and disputation are possible only when one is himself ignorant or involved with the ignorant, and the enlightened one is neither.

आशापाशविबन्धनमुक्ताः
शौचाचारविवर्जितयुक्ताः ।
एवं सर्वविवर्जितशान्त-
स्तत्त्वं शुद्धनिरञ्जनवन्तः ॥ ३ ॥

āśā-pāśa-vibandhana-muktāḥ
śaucācāra-vivarjita-yuktāḥ
evaṁ sarva-vivarjita-śāntaḥ
tattvaṁ śuddha-nirañjanavantaḥ.

3. Free from entrapment in the snares of hope and devoid of purificatory ceremonies,

the enlightened one is ever absorbed in the Absolute. Thus, having renounced all, he is the Truth, pure and stainless.

Purificatory, etc.—rules of purification of the body and mind, observed by the orthodox as part of religious discipline. The liberated do not need them and are above them.

कथमिह देहविदेहविचारः
कथमिह रागविरागविचारः ।
निर्मलनिश्चलगगनाकारं
स्वयमिह तत्त्वं सहजाकारम् ॥ ४ ॥

katham iha deha-videha-vicāraḥ
katham iha rāga-virāga-vicāraḥ
nirmala-niścala-gaganākāraṁ
svayam iha tattvaṁ sahajākāram.

4. How can there be any discussion here of body and disembodiment, of attachment and detachment? Here is the Truth Itself in Its spontaneous natural form—pure, immovable like the sky!

कथमिह तत्त्वं विन्दति यत्र
रूपमरूपं कथमिह तत्र ।
गगनाकारः परमो यत्र
विषयीकरणं कथमिह तत्र ॥ ५ ॥

katham iha tattvaṁ vindati yatra
rūpam arūpaṁ katham iha tatra
gaganākāraḥ paramo yatra
viṣayīkaraṇaṁ katham iha tatra.

5. Where the Truth is known, how can there be form or formlessness? Where there is the Supreme, whose form is like the sky, how is perception of any object possible?

How, etc.—The knower, knowledge, and known all become one in transcendental realization.

गगनाकारनिरन्तरहंस-
स्तत्त्वविशुद्धनिरञ्जनहंसः ।
एवं कथमिह भिन्नविभिन्नं
बन्धविबन्धविकारविभिन्नम् ॥ ६ ॥

gaganākara-nirantara-haṁsaḥ
tattva-viśuddha-nirañjana-haṁsaḥ
evaṁ katham iha bhinna-vibhinnaṁ
bandha-vibandha-vikāra-vibhinnam.

6. The supreme Self is indivisible, of the form of the sky. It is the Truth, pure and stainless. Thus, how can there be here difference and nondifference, bondage and freedom from bondage, transformation and division?

केवलतत्त्वनिरन्तरसर्वं
योगवियोगौ कथमिह गर्वम् ।

एवं परमनिरन्तरसर्वं-
मेव कथमिह सारविसारम् ॥ ७ ॥

kevala-tattva-nirantara-sarvaṁ
yoga-viyogau katham iha garvam
evaṁ parama-nirantara-sarvam
evaṁ katham iha sāra-visāram.

7. Here is only the absolute Truth, indivisible and the All. How can there be here union, disunion, or pride? If thus there is here only the Supreme, indivisible and the All, how can there be here any substance or absence of substance?

Pride—The ego dies on the realization of the Truth.

Substance—substance in a limited sense as the repository of qualities and therefore belonging to the relative plane.

केवलतत्त्वनिरञ्जनसर्वं
गगनाकारनिरन्तरशुद्धम् ।
एवं कथमिह सङ्गविसङ्गं
सत्यं कथमिह रङ्गविरङ्गम् ॥ ८ ॥

kevala-tattva-nirañjana-sarvaṁ
gaganākāra-nirantara-śuddham
evaṁ katham iha saṅga-visaṅgaṁ
satyaṁ katham iha raṅga-viraṅgam.

8. Here is the absolute Truth, indivisible and pure, stainless and the All, of the form of

the sky. Thus, how can there be here association and dissociation? How, truly, can there be here any play or cessation of play?

Play—enjoyment of relative life.

योगवियोगै रहितो योगी
भोगविभोगै रहितो भोगी ।
एवं चरति हि मन्दं मन्दं
मनसा कल्पितसहजानन्दम् ॥ ९ ॥

yoga-viyogaiḥ rahito yogī
bhoga-vibhogaiḥ rahito bhogī
evaṁ carati hi mandaṁ mandaṁ
manasā kalpita-sahajānandam.

9. The enlightened one is a yogī devoid of yoga and absence of yoga. He is an enjoyer, devoid of enjoyment and absence of enjoyment. Thus he wanders leisurely, filled with the spontaneous joy of his own mind.

Yòga—practice of concentration. The yogī who is enlightened has gone beyond the need for it.

Absence, etc.—because he is in the state of eternal yoga, or Self-realization.

Enjoyment, etc.—enjoyment of relative life. Absence of such enjoyment would imply self-restraint and self-abnegation. The enlightened one is beyond both.

बोधविबोधैः सततं युक्तो
द्वैताद्वैतैः कथमिह मुक्तः ।
सहजो विरजः कथमिह योगी
शुद्धनिरञ्जनसमरसभोगी ॥ १० ॥

bodha-vibodhaiḥ satataṁ yukto
dvaitādvaitaiḥ katham iha muktaḥ
sahajo virajaḥ katham iha yogī
śuddha-nirañjana-samarasa-bhogī.

10. If the yogī is always related to knowledge and perception, to duality and unity, how can he be free here? How can a yogī be natural and free from attachment here? He is the enjoyer of the pure, stainless, and homogeneous Being.

भग्नाभग्नविवर्जितभग्नो
लग्नालग्नविवर्जितलग्नः ॥
एवं कथमिह सारविसारः
समरसतत्त्वं गगनाकारः ॥ ११ ॥

bhagnābhagna-vivarjita-bhagno
lagnālagna-vivarjita-lagnaḥ
evaṁ katham iha sāra-visāraḥ
samarasa-tattvaṁ gaganākāraḥ.

11. The Self is Destruction, devoid of the destroyed and undestroyed. The Self is the Auspicious Moment, devoid of the auspicious

and inauspicious time. Thus, how can there be here substance and absence of substance? The Truth which is homogeneous is of the form of the sky.

Destruction—negation of all relative phenomena.

Destroyed, etc.—remnants of negated phenomena; "undestroyed"—phenomena still existing. "Destroyed" and "undestroyed" may also mean phenomena reduced to the undifferentiated form and phenomena in the differentiated state, which together constitute the universe.

Auspicious, etc.—Although the expression refers to time, eternity is really meant. It is called auspicious because the eternal Self is holy.

सततं सर्वविवर्जितयुक्तः
सर्वं तत्त्वविवर्जितमुक्तः ।
एवं कथमिह जीवितमरणं
ध्यानाध्यानैः कथमिह करणम् ॥ १२ ॥

satataṁ sarva-vivarjita-yuktaḥ
sarvaṁ tattva-vivarjita-muktaḥ
evaṁ katham iha jīvita-maraṇaṁ
dhyānādhyānaiḥ katham iha karaṇam.

12. Forever divested of all and united to the Self, the enlightened one is the All, free and devoid of truth. Thus, how can there be here life and death, and how can there be any

accomplishment through meditation or lack of meditation?

Devoid,etc.—devoid of relative truth.

Accomplishment, etc.—In the transcendental state, meditation is not possible.

इन्द्रजालमिदं सर्वं यथा मरुमरीचिका ।
अखण्डितमनाकारो वर्तते केवलः शिवः ॥ १३ ॥

indrajālam idaṁ sarvaṁ yathā marumarīcikā
akhaṇḍitam anākāro vartate kevalaḥ śivaḥ.

13. All this is magic, like a mirage in the desert. Only the absolute Self, of indivisible and impenetrable form, exists.

धर्मादौ मोक्षपर्यन्तं निरीहाः सर्वथा वयम् ।
कथं रागविरागैश्च कल्पयन्ति विपश्चितः ॥ १४ ॥

dharmādau mokṣa-paryantaṁ
nirīhāḥ sarvathā vayam
kathaṁ rāga-virāgaiś ca
kalpayanti vipaścitaḥ.

14. To all things, from the practice of religious laws and duties to liberation, we are completely indifferent. How can we have anything to do with attachment or detachment? Only the learned imagine these things.

Practice, etc.—The reference is to the fourfold idea of life as prescribed in Hinduism: dharma (observance of religious laws and duties for well-being here and hereafter); artha (acquisition of wealth); kāma (satisfaction of legitimate desires); and mokṣa (liberation).

We—the enlightened.

Learned—scholars without spiritual experience.

विन्दति विन्दति न हि न हि यत्र
छन्दोलक्षणं न हि न हि तत्र ।
समरसमग्नो भावितपूतः
प्रलपति तत्त्वं परमवधूतः ॥ १५ ॥

vindati vindati na hi na hi yatra
chando-lakṣaṇaṁ na hi na hi tatra
samarasa-magno bhāvita-pūtaḥ
pralapati tattvaṁ param avadhūtaḥ.

15. Where one knows nothing, there is verily no versification. The supreme and free One, pure of thought, absorbed in the consciousness of the homogeneous Being, prattles about the Truth.

CHAPTER VIII

त्वद्यात्रया व्यापकता हता ते
ध्यानेन चेतःपरता हता ते ।
स्तुत्या मया वाक्परता हता ते
क्षमस्व नित्यं त्रिविधापराधान् ॥ १ ॥

tvad-yātrayā vyāpakatā hatā te
dhyānena cetaḥ-paratā hatā te
stutyā mayā vākparatā hatā te
kṣamasva nityaṁ trividhāparādhān.

1. By my making pilgrimage to Thee Thy all-pervasiveness has been destroyed by me. With my meditation Thy transcendence of the mind has been destroyed by me. Thy transcendence of speech has been destroyed by me by my singing Thy praise. Ever forgive me these three sins.

Thee—to Thy shrines, temples, and holy places.

All-pervasiveness, etc.—To assume, as pilgrimage does, that the Divine Presence is particularly existent in certain shrines and temples is to deny that God is present everywhere equally.

Transcendence, etc.—In meditation God is contemplated in the mind, making God thereby mental, whereas God is beyond mind.

Transcendence, etc.—Singing the praise of God implies that God is within the range of speech, whereas He is beyond it.

कामैरहतधीर्दान्तो मृदुः शुचिरकिञ्चनः ।
अनीहो मितभुक् शान्तः स्थिरो मच्छरणो मुनिः ॥२॥

kāmair ahatadhīr dānto
mṛduḥ śucir akiñcanaḥ
anīho mita-bhuk śāntaḥ
sthiro maccharaṇo muniḥ.

2. A sage is one whose intelligence is unsmitten by lusts, who is self-controlled, gentle, and pure, who possesses nothing, who is indifferent, who eats moderately, is quiet and steady, and has taken refuge in Me.

Indifferent—to all relative things and states.
Me—the Self.

अप्रमत्तो गभीरात्मा धृतिमान् जितषड्गुणः ।
अमानी मानदः कल्पो मैत्रः कारुणिकः कविः ॥ ३ ॥

apramatto gabhīrātmā dhṛtimān jita-ṣaḍ-guṇaḥ
amānī mānadaḥ kalpo maitraḥ kāruṇikaḥ kaviḥ.

3. The sage is vigilant and resolute, has a profound mind, and has conquered the six

bondages; he is not proud, but gives honour to others; he is strong, friendly to all, compassionate, and wise.

Six,etc.—six passions, lust, anger, greed, infatuation: pride, and envy.

कृपालुरकृतद्रोहस्तितिक्षुः सर्वदेहिनाम् ।
सत्यसारोऽनवद्यात्मा समः सर्वोपकारकः ॥ ४ ॥

kṛpālurakṛta-drohaḥ titiksuh sarva-dehinām
satya-sāro anavadyātmā samaḥ sarvopakā-rakaḥ.

4. The sage is merciful, nonviolent, and enduring of all. He is pure-hearted and is the essence of truth; he is the same to all and beneficent to all.

अवधूतलक्षणं वर्णैर्ज्ञातव्यं भगवत्तमैः ।
वेदवर्णार्थतत्त्वज्ञैर्वेदवेदान्तवादिभिः ॥ ५ ॥

avadhūta-lakṣaṇaṁ varṇaiḥ
jñātavyaṁ bhagavattamaiḥ
veda-varṇārtha-tattvajñaiḥ.
veda-vedānta-vādibhiḥ.

5. The sign of an avadhūta should be known by the blessed ones, by those who know the truth of the significance of the letters of the Vedas and who teach Veda and Vedānta.

आशापाशविनिर्मुक्त आदिमध्यान्तनिर्मलः ।
आनन्दे वर्तते नित्यमकारं तस्य लक्षणम् ॥ ६ ॥

āśā-pāśa-vinirmuktaḥ ādi-madhyānta-nir
-malaḥ.
ānande vartate nityam akāraṁ tasya lakṣaṇam.

6. The significance of the letter "a" is that the avadhūta is free from the bondage of hopes, is pure in the beginning, middle, and end, and dwells ever in joy.

Hopes—desires.

वासना वर्जिता येन वक्तव्यं च निरामयम् ।
वर्तमानेषु वर्तेत वकारं तस्य लक्षणम् ॥ ७ ॥

vāsanā varjitā yena vaktavyaṁ ca nirāmayam
vartamāneṣu varteta vakāraṁ tasya lakṣaṇam.

7. The syllable "va" is indicative of him by whom all desires have been renounced, whose speech is wholesome, and who dwells in the present.

Dwells, etc.—because he is free from effects of past experience and does not indulge in hopes and expectations and, therefore, is free of the future.

धूलिधूसरगात्राणि धूतचित्तो निरामयः ।
धारणाध्याननिर्मुक्तो धूकारस्तस्य लक्षणम् ॥ ८ ॥

ḍhūli-dhūsara-gātrāṇi dhūta-citto nirāmayaḥ
dhāraṇā-dhyāna-nirmukto dhūkāras tasya lakṣaṇam.

8. The syllable "dhū" is a sign of him whose limbs are grey with dust, whose mind is purified, who is free of all diseases, and who is released from the practices of concentration and meditation.

Limbs—he does not mind where he sits or sleeps.

Released, etc.—All such spiritual practices imply ignorance and bondage, but he is free and illumined.

तत्त्वचिन्ता धृता येन चिन्ताचेष्टाविवर्जितः ।
तमोऽहंकारनिर्मुक्तस्तकारस्तस्य लक्षणम् ॥ ९ ॥

tattva-cintā dhṛtā yena cinta-ceṣtā-vivarjitaḥ
tamo'hankāra-nirmuktaḥ takāras tasya lakṣaṇam.

9. The syllable "ta" is significant of him by whom the thought of Truth has been made steady, who is devoid of all thoughts and efforts, and who is free from ignorance and egoism.

Thought, etc.—that is to say, Truth has been fully realized.

दत्तात्रेयावधूतेन निर्मितानन्दरूपिणा।
ये पठन्ति च शृण्वन्ति तेषां नैव पुनर्भवः ॥ १० ॥

dattātreyāvadhūtena nirmitānandarūpiṇā
ye paṭhanti ca śṛṇvanti teṣāṁ naiva punarbhavaḥ.

10. This Gītā or Song is composed by Dattātreya Avadhūta who is the embodiment of bliss. Whoever reads or hears it has never any rebirth.

Has, etc.—One who has realized the Self is never reborn.